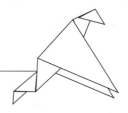

LEADING CHANGE:

*How Boards
and Presidents
Build Exceptional
Academic Institutions*

TERRENCE MACTAGGART

PRESS

Development of this book was generously supported by Lumina Foundation.

Leading Change: How Boards and Presidents Build Exceptional Academic Institutions

Library of Congress Cataloging-in-Publication Data

MacTaggart, Terrence J., 1946-

Leading change : How boards and presidents build exceptional academic institutions / Terrence J. MacTaggart.

    p. cm.

 ISBN 978-0-9754948-2-0

1. Public universities and colleges--United States--Administration--Case studies.
2. Higher education and state--United States--Case studies.
3. Educational change—United States--Case studies.
I. Title.

LB2341.M157 2011

378.73—dc23

                            2011017437

For more information on AGB Press publications or to order additional copies of this book, call 800/356-6317 or visit the AGB Web site at www.agb.org.

TABLE OF CONTENTS

FOREWORD

This book is about change and higher education. It offers snapshots of moments of change at 18 colleges, universities, and systems. While profound societal change is nothing new, today's unique combination of forces—economic, academic, demographic, global, technological, regulatory, and political—make this a pivotal point for our society and higher education. The last century was considered the "American Century," but we cannot presume the same as we move through the 21st century. Nationally and globally, higher education holds the greatest promise for addressing the challenges of the future.

This critical juncture requires us to meet a new set of challenges head-on. Change is affecting colleges and universities—public and independent, large and small institutions. The academy is confronting rising expectations as the nation seeks to expand access to higher education, close the achievement gap, increase attainment, and dramatically grow the number of degrees. The impact of the economic downturn and a noticeable decline in public trust complicate what we do and how we do it. Compounding the challenge, our traditional relationships with diverse constituencies are also evolving, as government and corporate sectors stake out their expectations. Clearly, different times require different ways of thinking.

Against this backdrop, the Association of Governing Boards of Universities and Colleges (AGB) sought to examine how higher-education institutions and systems tackled change—who recognized the need for change, how it was framed, and what role boards played in implementing it. Led by Terry MacTaggart, who continues to ask the right questions about the state of the academy, we explored a multitude of different types of changes—preemptive and reactive changes, internally driven and externally prompted changes, changes to improve upside potential and changes to manage downside risk. We wanted to understand how the board-president partnership worked during periods of change and to learn what governance practices supported boards in the midst of uncertainty and transition.

The genesis of this book stems from years of listening to academic leaders share their stories of change—change that was intentionally sought and change that was imposed upon them. They had to know when good enough was no longer good enough and when new directions required shifts in institutional practices. They had to know when long-held assumptions about educational quality were no longer valid and when traditional business models were no longer sustainable. In short, presidents, chancellors, and boards had to determine if, when, and to what extent their institution's future was in jeopardy. Along the way, they reassessed and adjusted their mission statements, strategies, and operations to current realities, sometimes modestly and other times substantially. Sometimes they succeeded, other times they struggled.

We peered under the hood of higher-education boards at these seminal moments: What was the board's role in the change? How did board members partner with the president? When and how do other stakeholders need to be involved? Why are some boards, including presidents and chancellors, able to navigate successfully through change? We greatly appreciate the 41 academic institutions and systems that welcomed our research team onto their campuses and into their offices and boardrooms. We learned much from the opportunities and access they provided us. This book could not have been written without the active support and transparency of these fine institutions. Their openness is a gift to all academic institutions and leaders.

In the end, we focused on the experiences of 18 colleges, universities, and systems. Through the lens of these actual examples, we captured freeze frames of institutions during moments of change. Each case study reveals a distinct story of what, how, and when the board engaged in institutional change. Some stories are drawn from threats to institutional survival; others relate to dramatic updrafts in institutional performance. Some are monumental turning points; others are less severe but no less complex, especially as they relate to board engagement.

One consistent theme we found was that change-adept boards worked in partnership with their chief executive officer on continuous improvement for the institution or system. We also found that change-adept boards challenged themselves to achieve a higher level of governance performance. The end goal was the same: stronger academic institutions. A constructive relationship between the president and board was an essential and positive factor in achieving real change.

In these stories, you may recognize elements of change relevant to the challenges confronting your own institution. Our role is part tour guide, part provocateur on this path of change. This volume offers board members, presidents, and chancellors case studies and lessons learned, principles and best practices, and tools and techniques grounded in firsthand experience. It shows how meaningful institutional change requires meaningful engagement of governing bodies in collaboration with chief executives and other academic leaders. This book is not intended to move boards into institutional management. Rather, it reveals those moments in an institution's life that raise core questions whose responses fundamentally change the college or university. It is in this space that boards must engage and be engaged.

Ultimately, this is a book about how governing boards can and should effect significant change within their institutions, change that is often required in pursuit of excellence. We appreciate the support provided by Lumina Foundation for this research initiative. Its commitment to strengthening higher education is laudable and challenging. We at AGB are proud to join it in pursuit of this goal.

Change is rarely easy for us as individuals, and that much more complicated for large, complex institutions. When viewed from the boardroom—an essential part of the campus community, but inhabited by those who are not physically part of the campus on a daily basis—it can be especially daunting. The path forward may not be apparent, and the role of the board often seems ambiguous. But change in higher education is inevitable, and success requires intentional and thoughtful board engagement.

Richard D. Legon
President
Association of Governing Boards of Universities and Colleges
July 2011

PREFACE

"Nothing endures but change."
~ Heraclitus (540 – 480 BC)

This book is dedicated to every board member and president of a college or university who has faced a turning point in their institution's trajectory. They may have asked themselves what it would take to enable their institution to rise to the next level. They may have been navigating a planned leadership transition or the fallout of a scandal. They may have confronted a steady decline in enrollment or a sudden financial shortfall. Whatever the circumstances and root causes, the solution involved change, and that change took place through a process and over time. In the most-constructive and productive instances, the board and the president led the change process together.

This book explores what change entails for the board of a particular college, university, or public system of universities at a pivotal time in its history. It examines the intersection of three core components of change:

- Institutional progress, be it recovery from a decline or crisis, the climb to higher levels of excellence, or the combination of these;
- Leadership, including inspiration, vision, and stewardship; and
- The interdependence of governance and management, boards and presidents.

This book offers models and practical tools for building a change-adept board.

Change Comes in Many Shapes

Change has a multitude of factors that fall across a spectrum, from preemptive to reactive, from internally to externally induced, from incremental to radical. To guide an institution through any kind of transition, the board and president must first determine the kind of change required of them.

Institutions that aspire to become substantially better can do so in several ways. One way is to become the best in their league, be they a private research university, a public land-grant institution, a regional comprehensive university, a community college, or a school with a highly specialized mission. Improved educational effectiveness—measured by high retention and graduation rates, scores on student-engagement surveys, and benchmarks of student success—is another. Potential targets for aspiring institutions and boards are many. Selecting the right one turns out to be a difficult task.

Institutions that must respond to a crisis confront a different set of alternatives. In these instances, a turnaround is in order. The challenge here is to restore financial integrity, build or rebuild a tarnished reputation, revise the operational model to restore marketability, and often reinvigorate the academic program. Change-adept boards, especially those with members versed in business turnarounds, often initiate the transformations required to recover from a crisis.

Boards and Change

This book focuses on board behaviors and actions that contribute mightily to positive institutional change. But to understand these transformational moments, we must look at both the impetus for the change and at the leaders who push and pull the institution through the change process. In higher education, leadership involves not just the president and professionals, but also volunteer board members. Traditionally, the literature and practice of governance emphasize fiduciary oversight and institutional advancement. The board's role and appropriate parameters in prompting, navigating, enabling, and supporting change has been, at best, a secondary consideration.

Based on an AGB research study funded by Lumina Foundation, this book stands apart from what has gone before. First, we focus on the dynamics of board perceptions and actions that lead to positive institutional change. To be sure, other researchers do not ignore linkages between board action and institutional results. Yet, they concentrate on recommended board behaviors, while assuming that superior practice will inevitably lead to better results.

We sought to be highly empirical by looking first to institutions that experienced positive change, then working backward to the role the board played in bringing about that change. We excluded institutions that experienced marvelous change in which the board played little role. Our focus on cases where the board made a demonstrable difference enables us to offer lessons learned from the work of real boards bringing positive change to their institutions. We have looked to board actions that have both exemplified and defied conventional best practices to get to the true, underlying best practices of change-adept boards.

Second, we cast a wide net to capture a variety of boards and institutions. Most of the literature of governance focuses on boards of private liberal arts colleges. The implicit judgment here is that "the best public boards act like private ones." We believe instead that the underlying principles of superior trusteeship are the same for both. Although public boards hold only a portion of the authority of their independent counterparts, adroitly used, that fraction can yield enormous results. Because they have the potential to improve the quality and availability of education for literally hundreds of thousands of students, boards of public systems of colleges and universities can be especially influential.

Third, we concentrated on board performance at a truly superior level that resulted in an institution improving in some notable way. In some instances, the board led a dramatic turnaround following on the heels of a fall from grace. In others, farsighted board leaders came to believe that the current level of board and institutional performance was simply not good enough to address the host of competitive pressures. Thanks to increasingly sophisticated and more widely distributed literature on effective trusteeship, greater federal and state attention to the fiduciary responsibilities of boards, and the talent of committed board members, average trusteeship has improved over the last two decades. This progress in performance has created an appetite among board members and presidents for taking governance to the next level.

Research Methodology

We selected colleges and universities for our research study based on two fundamental questions: Did the college or university experience substantial change? Did the board play a major role in initiating and sustaining that change? Of course, a third question shaped our efforts: Would the institution give us unfettered access to meetings and documents related to these questions?

After a pilot project that studied five institutions, we solicited self-nominations and suggestions from an advisory group, identifying 41 institutions. We winnowed this group down to 22 institutions and conducted telephone interviews. We were especially interested in boards that had sustained an important trajectory through the tenure of two or more presidencies, although that was not a litmus test for participation.

We selected 12 colleges and universities for site visits. During those visits, members of the research team interviewed the president and former president (if available), current and former board leaders, long-term staff and faculty members, and regulators familiar with the institution—such as accrediting agency executives. In most cases, a team member also observed board and committee meetings. We then followed up with additional phone interviews to get more depth and detail on the board's role in bringing about positive change. Team members summarized their findings and conclusions in a written report.

We also sought diversity among types of institutions to see if our conclusions carried across different settings. We interviewed system chief executives, board members, and campus administrators in three public higher-education systems. Ultimately, we found that the paths to institutional change—regardless of the type of institution—were more similar than not. The talents of individual leaders and a mastery of the art and management of change were the most important factors.

Who Should Read This Book

In this book, we address the issue of institutional change from multiple perspectives—board members, presidents, faculty leaders, donors, students, and policy makers. The ideas in this book will enable presidents to become more successful by collaborating with their deeply engaged boards. It will guide boards and chairs in nurturing more involved board members, exercising governance discipline while asserting board leadership, and working more effectively with their presidents to advance their institutions. Legislators and governors who influence higher-education appropriations and policy will learn how public board members and their executives contribute to the prosperity of their states through distinctive colleges and universities, and high-functioning systems of higher education. Faculty leaders will find new ways to interact with board members. And students of governance will encounter new approaches and different perspectives on the role of the board.

Chapter-by-Chapter Summary

Grounded in the experiences of 18 colleges and universities, this book brings together management theory and best practices related to change, organizational leadership, and board governance. Using higher education as the locus of attention, it offers lessons learned for overcoming obstacles and strengthening board-president relationships in the midst of notable transitions. The appendix presents brief case studies of each institution. Each chapter includes lessons learned from several institutions and discussion questions for board and administrative leaders.

Chapter 1 presents the challenges and dilemmas facing institutions of higher education: the increasingly competitive global workforce, the financial realities of the 21st century, and heightened scrutiny of governance practices, among others. Chapter 2 looks at different prompts and circumstances of change. It also presents the various kinds of change—operational, behavioral, and adaptive—and common obstacles to change.

Chapters 3, 4, and 5 examine the respective roles, responsibilities, and relationships of the president and board. Chapter 3 focuses on the board-president partnership that is essential to effective institutional governance and management. It explores issues related to trust and decision making, as well as the impediments to this leadership partnership. Chapter 4 digs into the board's role, prerequisites, and readiness for change. Chapter 5 offers guidance to presidents for nurturing and supporting their board's capacity for change.

Chapter 6 looks more closely at board composition and outlines techniques for strategic recruitment of board members who will contribute to positive change. It makes the case for genuine board self-assessment, as well as more sophisticated and substantive board education and succession planning.

Chapters 7 and 8 draw on the experiences of systems and institutions that have climbed up the ladder. Chapter 7 focuses on developing change-adept system boards that can balance state priorities with room for innovation by campus boards and presidents. Chapter 8 draws the connection between aspiring boards and aspiring institutions by tapping into the lessons learned from six very different colleges and universities that have risen to the next level of quality and performance.

We fully appreciate the unique circumstances of each institution, and we recognize the differences between independent and public institutions, liberal arts colleges, and comprehensive research universities, to name a few. For the purpose of this book, we have chosen the most common vernacular of academe. For example, the board is comprised of board members, rather than trustees or regents. The president, rather than the chancellor or chief executive, refers to the highest-ranking professional who leads the institution or system. This was done for convenience, not as a recommendation.

Next-Level Board Performance

Having completed a first level or two of board development, a growing number of presidents and chairs turn to the Association of Governing Boards for advanced board-development opportunities. In many cases, an institutional crisis—either self-inflicted or growing from the relentlessly competitive market for students, faculty members, and resources—has led board members to seek ways to become more effective. Likewise, more and more presidents recognize that an "all hands on deck" approach to leadership, especially during pivotal moments, will benefit their institutions. By working in partnership with an able and engaged board, their college or university can more readily reach the next level of accomplishment and success.

Everyone who believes that boards are central to navigating institutional change and improving our nation's colleges and universities will find value in this book. This includes leaders of public as well as independent institutions, of single campus colleges and multicampus systems. We seek to help these audiences better understand how truly exceptional board performance can help build and sustain exceptional academic institutions.

Acknowledgments

Like most good ideas, the framework for the Governance for Student Success project that led to this volume and the structure of the book itself were the product of a collective effort. I appreciate the contributions and support of many gifted partners and organizations to this book. First is the Association of Governing Boards and especially its president, Rick Legon, who initially envisioned a study of the role of boards in leading and guiding change.

Susan Whealler Johnston, AGB executive vice president, was the driving force behind the research project and my partner-in-crime for a series of related workshops. Ellen Earl Chaffee, AGB senior fellow and consultant extraordinaire, was an adept project director, invaluable interviewer, and critical reader. Back at the office, Kyle Long, former AGB project associate, helped coordinate our research efforts. During the earliest stages of this study, we tapped into a seasoned and sage advisory group that included Kent Chabotar, Judith McLaughlin, David Roberts, and Barbara Taylor.

On behalf of AGB, I want to thank Lumina Foundation for its ongoing commitment to enabling many more Americans to achieve a college degree, strengthening America's system of higher education, and recognizing the important role volunteer board members play in our colleges and universities.

On behalf of the research team, I want to extend our heartfelt thanks to the college and university leaders—presidents and chancellors, board members, and administrative staff—who participated in this project. They were generous with their time, open about the challenges and the rewards of their experiences, and insightful in their commentary about change and leadership.

Readers will observe that many of the ideas on change in this book originated from the seminal minds of Jim Collins, Ronald Heifetz, George Keller and John Kotter, among others. With respect to thinking about governance in business and higher education, we are indebted to the works of Richard Chait, Barbara Taylor, Thomas Holland, William Ryan, Robert Berdahl, Adrian Tinsley, Tom Ingram, Dick Richardson, Richard Novak, David Nadler, and Jeffrey Sonnenfeld, among others.

Finally, this book benefited from the talents and persistence of three superb editors, Marla J. Bobowick, Ellen ("the editor") Hirzy, and Sarah Hardesty Bray.

Terrence MacTaggart
July 2011

Chapter 1

THE NEED FOR CHANGE-ADEPT BOARDS

To govern a college or university in today's complicated environment often means to lead change. Consider these examples:

- After cutting the budget for three years, seeing more students they wanted to attract heading elsewhere, and sensing steadily deteriorating faculty and staff morale, the board members of Oberlin College took action to avert the decline of this nationally recognized liberal arts college and conservatory. They began by engaging with the president in an institution-wide strategic planning effort that would involve virtually all members of the campus community and ultimately restore Oberlin's competitive position as a top national liberal arts institution.

- Board members at Hendrix College, one of Arkansas' premier liberal arts colleges, observed a perfect storm headed their way. A change in state financial-aid policy meant a potentially significant decline in net tuition revenue, and a $300-million gift to a nearby state university promised greater competition for the state's best students. The board partnered with the new president and faculty members on a strategy for building programs and a campus environment that would sustain the college's place in the competitive world of private higher education.

- The University System of Maryland confronted declining state aid, rising costs in energy and health care, growing enrollment, and greater demands for higher education in a knowledge-based economy. It examined its operations from top to bottom, with the goal of improving and maintaining quality, despite limited funding. The board launched the Effectiveness and Efficiency Initiative, which led to higher teaching loads, a tuition freeze, and improved access, while retaining quality.

- The newly established board of Metropolitan State College of Denver was determined to make the college a major player in regional growth, to pioneer novel public-private partnerships in support of that growth, and to enroll many more minority, especially Hispanic, students. They hired a new president to work with them in leading the change, and as a result Metro State emerged as a premier urban public baccalaureate institution.

These narratives of change share a two-part theme: an energetic engagement of the board with the college or university and a productive partnership with the president. Instead of maintaining an almost single-minded focus on fiscal oversight, these boards are comfortable in a holistic, strategic role that involves governing, leading, and monitoring results through periods of change. Their members often bring a perspective from the business world, where constant change in response to relentless competition is the order of the day. At the same time, they are aware of and educated about the specific concerns of higher education, and how it differs from business.

They ask the right questions about their institution's performance and its ability to attract, retain, and graduate students, the trends in its financial position, the sustainability of its current operational model, and the like. They insist on change and become involved in the change process when they see a necessary and appropriate role for the board. This governance model still demands strict attention to protecting the institution's assets. But it also incorporates a complementary commitment to educational quality, which requires change to strengthen the college or university and improve its academic effectiveness.

This chapter highlights the following issues:

- Why higher education needs change to achieve stronger institutions, higher academic quality, and better educational performance;
- How boards can assert positive change leadership;
- What approaches to change leadership can enhance the board's exercise of its fiduciary, policymaking, and strategic responsibilities; and
- What questions board members should ask themselves before embarking on a change process.

Why Higher Education Must Change

Why change? There are compelling reasons: to better prepare our students for a globally competitive society, to strengthen our colleges and universities both financially and academically, and to give far more of our citizens the skills an advanced society needs. It is no secret that the emerging economies of China, India, Brazil, and a host of smaller countries are overtaking the United States in economic vitality. In a world where knowledge is the essential strategic resource, we must develop the best-educated citizenry at the most-effective institutions if we are to sustain a high-wage economy. The alternative is a steady decline in our standard of living, fewer opportunities for social mobility, and the dimming of the American dream.

Many colleges and universities need to change, either to reverse a gentle glide into mediocrity or simply to survive. Smaller, private four-year colleges, according to Moody's Investors Services, are at particular risk of declining quality and attractiveness to students because they are unable to stand up to the competition for enrollment and resources. Consider the realities facing board members at colleges and universities that Moody's describes as "too small to succeed":

- Eighty percent of ratings downgrades occur at private colleges.
- Private colleges have more Aaa ratings than other sectors, but they also have more ratings of Baa and below.
- Nearly half of all private four-year colleges enroll fewer than 1,000 full-time students, while only 6 percent of their public competitors are that small.[1]

---

[1] Financial Outlook, U.S. Private Higher Education, National Association of Independent College and University State Executives (NAICUSE) Summer Meeting, July 26–27, 2010.

Such statistics should serve as a wakeup call, if one is needed. Smaller colleges without a distinctive niche face a harsh reality: Change for the better or risk decline and possibly going out of business.

Even relatively well-financed and highly regarded institutions feel their competitors closing in on or surpassing them in the race for more money, better students and faculty members, and a reputation as an exceptionally valuable educational choice. For example, the internationally recognized Thunderbird School of Global Management faced falling enrollment and sharply declining revenues as a result of stiffer competition as well as in the aftermath of the September 11, 2001, terrorist attacks. The board and faculty changed how the institution operated, finding a sustainable equilibrium between what it cost to deliver a high-quality business education and what students were willing to pay for it.

The Competitive Global Environment and Other Challenges

While colleges and universities face the need to improve academic quality and boost educational and operational effectiveness, a parallel reality confronts the nation as a whole. Only a few decades ago, the United States led the world in the percentage of its workforce holding two- or four-year degrees. Yet today, only about 40 percent of the 25- to 34-year-old cohort has more than a high-school diploma, leaving the United States in 10th place behind better-educated developed countries, according to a report from the Organisation for Economic Co-operation and Development (OECD). Lumina Foundation reports that "rates of college degree attainment are increasing in almost every OECD country faster than in the United States." The foundation, which has adopted the closing of this educational-attainment gap as its key priority, points out that educational shortfalls go beyond slippage in the global rankings. Consider these statistics:

- While more than one-third of white, non-Hispanic, American adults has at least four years of college, only 18 percent of African Americans and 12 percent of Hispanics are in this category.
- Income gaps between better-educated majority students and less-well-educated minorities are exacerbated because on average a four-year degree delivers an income of $43,000, while a high-school diploma offers just $27,000—along with a much higher rate of unemployment.
- Unless more Americans achieve higher degrees, there is apt to be a shortage of 23 million college-educated adults by 2025 because of the growing demand for workers with advanced education.
- Without substantial acceleration of graduation rates, the gap between the educational attainment of the workforce and the demands of the economy will persist.

Who will assert the kind of leadership that is essential to reversing such ominous trends? To be sure, leadership from federal and state governments as well as college and university presidents is essential to a turnaround. But boards, which hold ultimate responsibility for delivering educational value, should not sit idly by while their institutions and the nation's human capital diminish in comparison to our global competitors. Meanwhile, many less visible but no less dangerous trends also call for action. Among the compelling challenges that confront most public and private institutions are the underfunded reserves for such things as deferred maintenance and employee health care and retirement, the failure to improve faculty teaching productivity, lagging investment returns, and stagnant or near-stagnant fund-raising levels.

Heightened Governance Standards

Sometimes what needs to be changed is not the institution or its operations, but its leadership structure and practices. The board role now requires greater fiscal oversight, better understanding of strategy and organizational capacity, and deeper engagement. Scandals attributed in part to lax governance represent an additional pressure for boards to become more engaged in change, especially in their own governance behaviors.

The Sarbanes-Oxley Act of 2002, familiarly known as SOX, was a response to the board oversight scandals at Enron and other high-flying companies. While SOX did not apply specifically to nonprofit institutions, it did contribute to a new culture of vigilance among boards with respect to fiscal integrity, risk management, and presidential and institutional performance. Board members with business backgrounds were especially inclined to bring such higher standards to academic institutions through more-focused use of the annual audit, closer attention to the Form 990, and greater vigilance around conflicts of interest. In this new climate, boards have taken a series of short, logical steps, from increased financial oversight to more interest in institutional performance to board engagement in the change process.

Within higher-education circles, well-publicized scandals that first focused on exorbitant presidential salaries grew to include board shortcomings. Lapses in the oversight of executive compensation at places like Adelphi University in New York in 1997 and American University in Washington, D.C., in 2005 sent a clear message that change should begin with dramatically improved governance practices.

How Boards Contribute to Change

The board is part of the university, not an appendage. The university is a circle with many unique pieces, including the trustees. They must be integrally involved. They must be engaged so that they can take the institution through a series of presidencies.

—CHARLES R. MIDDLETON, President, Roosevelt University

Without active board leadership, much critical change simply will not occur or will fall short of its goals. The board-president relationship is the essential one in moving the institution to a better place, and in any transformation involving teaching and learning, the faculty is a key partner. But as the cases in this book illustrate, change generally will not happen if the board is not an active contributor.

In independent colleges and universities, boards are the ultimate governing authority. At public colleges, universities, and systems, boards bring substantial heft to the change process through the sizeable delegated authority the state bestows on them. Especially when change threatens to destabilize time-honored ways of doing business and unsettle powerful stakeholder groups like faculty or alumni, a strong board is the backstop to ensure that change moves forward.

Thoughtful boards engage in different ways with their presidents to bring about positive change (see Chapter 4). Some board contributions to change derive from its intellectual capital, and some flow from its governance authority. There is a difference between the two. Board input based on the intelligence and experience of its members can help to form a fresh vision for the institution; focus attention on the most critical challenges; critique the prevailing wisdom from the vantage point of knowledgeable outsiders; bring new perspective, often from the business world; and illuminate old problems.

A board's contribution to change based on its formal power can take many forms, including regular monitoring of progress, or lack thereof; galvanizing others to take action; making tough decisions, especially when the institution is divided over which option to choose; saying no to recommendations that the board feels are inconsistent with the mission or are simply misguided; endorsing change in official statements and proclamations; and confirming in formal board actions the new order of things, whether a revised business model, a new curriculum, or a shift in budget priorities. The application of board authority works best when the board supports good ideas that have been developed through dialogue within the board and with other stakeholders. The combination of sound thinking and the board's formal authority can make the crucial difference between talking about change and taking action.

The remarkable change at Hendrix College, an independent college in Arkansas, would not have been as complete or successful if board members had not decisively met the "perfect storm" of less state student aid and more-intense competition from a nearby state institution (see Chapter 4). At Widener University, when a posse of disgruntled faculty criticized the new president's initiative to build a more socially engaged campus, the board informed the dissidents that the president was carrying out its wishes (see Chapter 3).

High-performing boards in public-sector institutions don't wait for politicians to take the initiative. Under the leadership of an especially tenacious chair, Clifford M. Kendall, the University System of Maryland Board of Regents embarked on an effectiveness and efficiency initiative that reduced costs while educating more students, increased teaching loads, ensured minimal tuition hikes, and, not incidentally, led to some funding increases from the Maryland General Assembly (see Chapter 7). Boards of public systems in North Carolina, Wisconsin, and other states are also engaged in ambitious change plans aimed at marshalling higher education's resources in support of more jobs at higher wages. In these instances, positive change emerged from a combination of compelling ideas for improving systemwide effectiveness and the board's statutory authority.

Change Leadership and Good Governance

The shift in our understanding of governance, from presiding over the institution to sometimes leading change, prompts several questions. As boards engage actively in galvanizing change or in the change process itself, do they risk losing the appropriate distance for fiduciary oversight? Does immersion in change blur the lines between the realms of president and board, between management and policy? Do board members have the interest, time, knowledge, and talent to contribute constructively to change at higher-education institutions? Or will they just in get in the way, leading to widespread dissatisfaction?

The institutions studied for this book show that boards can become bold actors in bringing change without endangering their enduring roles as fiduciaries and strategists. While not all boards have members with the time or inclination to lead change, many do—or they can be persuaded that deeper engagement in building a better institution is worth the extra time and effort. The new standard for high-performing governance expands the traditional notion to include helping the college or university change for the better.

Change Leadership as a Companion to Fiduciary Responsibility

There is a "new normal" for most colleges and universities that will mean more intense competition for students, donor support, and, at public institutions, government subsidies. It will also feature limits on increasing revenues through tuition hikes. In response to these realities, the concept of the board's fiduciary responsibility must include not only a glance in the rearview mirror at past financial performance, but a serious look forward at alternative scenarios. Some are grim indeed. This deeper fiduciary role combines strategic thinking and planning with the examination of trends and projections that will help the board anticipate future challenges. It may also mean that boards will need to better understand their institution's context and become more engaged in leading change, whatever form that change may take.

The traditional fiduciary role—holding the institution in trust for stakeholders ranging from students, to alumni, to faculty, to society at large—frequently demands that board members roll up their sleeves to become involved in the change process. The University of Dubuque in Iowa probably would have gone under if board members had not committed themselves and their resources to a turnaround of the beleaguered institution (see Chapter 8). With its large Coca-Cola holdings, Agnes Scott College likely would have survived as a business entity, but its plunging enrollments would have meant a diminished academic experience for students and faculty members. The incisive board action that halted and then reversed the decline illustrates a board carrying out its trust responsibility to preserve educational integrity (see Chapter 8).

In the abstract and in concrete situations, engaging in change appears to complement rather than conflict with fiduciary responsibility. Some boards have developed more-sophisticated financial models to identify costs and predict future trends. Far from abandoning their responsibility for fiduciary oversight, they have become more adept at using financial analysis to shape the direction of change.

The newer vision of the board's role equates responsible governance with two apparently contradictory perspectives. On the one hand, boards have adopted a much more engaged governance model. Board members are intent on understanding the institution that they govern and are focused on improving its performance. This approach inevitably leads to more personal interaction with management on strategy and its implementation. At the same time—and here is the paradox—boards maintain a greater sense of distance from their executives and display a greater willingness to expect more from them. This emerging relationship between the college or university board and president is bifocal. The board works more closely with the president in bringing change while standing apart to appraise his or her performance and, when necessary, set the bar higher. Boards contribute to positive change as a way of strengthening the institutions they govern and improving their educational quality and effectiveness.

Initiating and Guiding Change

The traditional boundaries between the board's policy role and the chief executive's operational role overlap in a number of instances, but especially in the face of change. New and different partnerships between the board and the president emerge from greater board involvement in a change process. In many of the institutions AGB studied, the board and the president were both heavily involved in initiating change and shared varying degrees of responsibility for guiding the change.

Figure 1.1 The Role of the Board in the Change Process

PRIMARY RESPONSIBILITY

	Initiating Change	Guiding Change	Ongoing Management
Board and President	Focus attention on problem or crisis and need for change		
President, Board, and Academic Community		Joint work on strategic directions; changes in business model; academic priorities	
Academic Community			Implementing new academic programs; on-line degrees, etc.

CHANGE TIMELINE

The model depicted in Figure 1.1 about the role of the president and board in change is a common but hardly universal one. Others include the hiring of a new president who subsequently galvanizes change at the institution, while essentially bringing the board along in the process. And occasionally, it is the faculty who capture the attention of a passive board with a no confidence vote, or the threat of one, in the executive, the board, or both. In these instances, the board should become actively engaged in the change process even though they do not initiate it.

Board Readiness for Change

Not all boards are cut out for change work. A small number of boards really do not want change, though they may not be willing to admit it. They may be wedded to the past, determined to preserve the way things always have been done, or losing interest in the long-term vitality of the institution they supposedly hold in trust. Other boards are dominated by powerful cliques of board members, each with its own agenda and priorities—for example, athletics or regional economic development over educational program. Resistance to change comes from these groups' desire to preserve control and advance their interests.

Boards can be described as primarily change-averse, change-adept, or change-prone (see Chapter 4). A key purpose of AGB's research was to discover how to move a board from averse or prone to become a change-adept board. Chapter 6 presents several models of good practice for developing a willing board into a change-adept one.

There are legitimate conditions when the decision not to change—or to limit the board's role in change—is the right decision. When a major change initiative is being implemented, the board should monitor the change and be attentive to unanticipated consequences, but hesitate to start another change initiative. At large institutions, especially research universities, public colleges, and state systems, the board is apt to be engaged in the early stage of galvanizing the change process, with substantially less involvement in its actual implementation. In rare instances an institution's market position may be so strong, its mission so secure and attractive, and its finances so stable that the board's chief role is monitoring the metrics to ensure that the well-oiled machine continues to operate smoothly. Even rarer is an institution with plenty of money and few or no competitive threats. Some boards define their role as strictly fiduciary and believe that change is the administration's responsibility. But the examples given at the beginning of this chapter suggest that had these boards abstained from playing an active role in change, their institutions would have been in far worse shape.

Real readiness for change involves a deep commitment. Board chairs who are effectively engaged in change, in particular, spend significant time partnering with their presidents and fellow board members on change work. Three change-adept chairs—Clifford M. Kendall of the University System of Maryland, David W. Oskin of Widener University, and Robert S. Lemle of Oberlin College—report that they devoted roughly half to all of their time at the height of the change process to their board leadership roles. Board members who are willing and able to understand what their institutions need, to devote the time, to learn what changing complex institutions is all about, and to recruit new members who share the same dedication can transform themselves into effective contributors to positive change.

A willing group of board members at the University of North Florida, led by its chairman, R. Bruce Taylor, was dedicated to building their capacity to guide change (see Chapter 8). Taylor encouraged his colleagues to reorganize committees and nearly double their time on task in order, in his words, to "support the president in taking this institution to the next level." The board studied the university's performance metrics on graduation rates, test scores, and other aspects of educational effectiveness. They compared its performance with that of peer institutions they wanted to emulate. At a lengthy retreat, board members queried regional employers on the qualities they sought in graduates, and then they asked deans to describe how the university worked to meet employer expectations.

Topics for Board and President Discussion

This chapter has made the case for greater board involvement in change. But how much does this argument apply to your institution? How willing and ready is your board to become involved in positive change? Raise the following questions to help your board decide whether a transition from a presiding board to an engaged board is appropriate and possible.

1. ***Institutional needs.*** What kind of change, if any, does our institution need? Is the change primarily an operational one that the board should oversee but leave to the good offices of the administration? Or is the change a far-reaching one affecting the mission and traditional business model that will require great and astute attention from the board? If the later, how well does the board understand the problem and how well prepared is it to contribute to the change?

2. ***Context and competition.*** Do we understand our institution's competitive position? The major threats and challenges it faces? The trends in its performance compared with the past and with similar institutions? If change is a process of moving from the current state to something better, can we define in concrete terms what "better" would look like?

3. ***Consequences of no change.*** What are the consequences if we do not engage in a change process? Will our institution go under, be diminished, or experience serious damage if change is ignored or unsuccessful? Will we continue to muddle through, and is that the best we can reasonably expect? Is our goal to move from pretty good to very good or even truly excellent? What is the likely outcome if we do nothing?

4. ***Leadership capacity.*** As a board and as individual board members, are we able and willing to work with our president to bring about positive change? Do enough of our members know about the change process in a complex institution to add value to this process? Can we develop that expertise, and are we willing to take the time to do so? Are we disciplined enough to honor the appropriate boundaries between the board and the executive during a change experience that promises to blur those boundaries? Can we return to our respective roles after the process is completed?

5. ***Change process and players.*** Based on this discussion, what is the right role for this board to play at this time? Should we encourage or require the president to initiate the change process? What kind of change do we want—incremental or transformational? At what pace should change occur? How will we monitor progress?

Chapter 2

THE POSITIVE POWER OF CHANGE

Change—and not just sporadic change at the margins—is necessary in just about every enterprise. Corporate and nonprofit leaders alike must be consistent and vigilant about improving performance and staying ahead of the competition, whether they are vying for customers, clients, parishioners, recognition, or financial support. The same holds true for boards and presidents of colleges and universities. It is no overstatement to say that to lead is to lead change—not change for the sake of change, but change to raise the institution's impact.

Sometimes the alternative is extinction. Some small colleges, unable to meet crises of enrollment and finances, have closed or been taken over by entrepreneurial for-profit educational businesses—not for the colleges' intrinsic value but for the cloak of accreditation they wear. If these trends persist, smaller, less-competitive institutions that lack a special niche will go out of existence or be swallowed up by larger, better-financed competitors.

The threat to most institutions is not extinction but the menace of mediocrity. Some liberal arts colleges find themselves dipping deeper into the applicant pool to accept less-well-prepared students in order to meet revenue needs. Research universities, especially in the public sector, find it increasingly difficult to amass the resources to hire and keep the best faculty members and to provide the laboratories, technology, and graduate students they need to sustain cutting-edge research. Even highly endowed elite institutions cannot take it for granted that aggressive upstarts won't threaten their advantage when it comes to attracting the best students and faculty members. Community colleges and regional universities, where the vast majority of undergraduate students enroll, risk being overwhelmed by the sheer numbers of those whom they must educate with fewer public dollars. The goal of graduating more well-educated students in a timely way remains elusive, as applicant numbers climb and dollars shrink.

The good news is that leaders, especially presidents and boards, have found ways to partner in taking their institutions in positive directions. They seize upon the energy generated by crises to bring about change. Or, absent a compelling crisis, they use indicators of flagging performance or forecasts of a dismal future to fuel a sense of urgency about change. Some board leaders act, and lead others to act, on the simple belief that "we can do better."

This chapter draws from some of those success stories to enlighten board members, both veterans and novices, who sense that their institutions need to change but wonder how to go about it. As a primer on bringing positive change to the academy, it introduces principles and ideas that are developed in later chapters. It addresses the following questions:

- What inspires a board to consider change in the institution?
- What kinds of change do colleges and universities face? How can boards appreciate the depth of change the institution needs?
- How can boards understand what is required of them in bringing about constructive change?
- What stands in the way of positive change in colleges and universities?

Three principal examples illustrate the board's powerful role in exercising change leadership: American University, where the board reformed its own governance practices in response to a crisis; Northern Kentucky University, where the board and president are leading an enterprise-wide adjustment to the "new normal" of declining state support and growing demand from the metropolitan Northern Kentucky–Cincinnati area; and Northwestern Health Sciences University, where flat enrollments and changes in health-care delivery led the board to expand the mission from chiropractic study to a model that integrates allopathic care with complementary and alternative forms of medicine.

Inducements to Change

In some situations, the message about needing board leadership for change flashes like a neon sign. In others, the warnings are muted, available only to more-alert minds attuned to telltale indications of worse things to come. Inducements to change tend to fall into three categories: a crisis; warning signs about past and future performance; and the visionary impulse to improve academic quality, student learning, or institutional reputation.

While change triggers may be separated for the purpose of analysis, in practice they usually occur in combination. Competition from other institutions and a change in student demand have led more than one college to the edge of bankruptcy or beyond. Measures showing low and declining graduation rates often accompany metrics suggesting that the negative trends will continue. Northern Kentucky University, for example, was not in an immediate crisis, but the board and the president realized that a crisis was not far off if they did not adjust the institution's operational model. This growing metropolitan university needed to make comprehensive changes in the way it conducted business if it were to continue its momentum in spite of significant reductions in its state appropriation. At Thunderbird School of Global Management in Glendale, Ariz., the catastrophe that occurred on the east coast on September 11, 2001, led to enrollment and financial reverses as international students were denied visas to study in the United States. Forecasts of continuing enrollment decline impelled the board to make fundamental changes in the financial model to accommodate new realities.

Crisis

A crisis is the most powerful inducement for change, and the most common. Many crises are occasioned by lapses in presidential or board attention. The failure to discern that the chief financial officer is no longer up to the task may lead to nasty surprises when the auditors visit. More than one board has underestimated the power of a new competitor, such as a low-cost community college or an entrepreneurial for-profit, to pull away students and resources. Whatever its cause, catastrophe breeds opportunity. The sense of urgency that accompanies a dramatic and well-publicized reversal is a powerful lever for change.

At American University, widely publicized charges of excessive spending for personal purposes led to the president's departure. The scandal prompted national headlines, a Congressional investigation, and threats of government action that set off alarms in the boardroom. Board leaders responded to the immediate problems, but they also used them as a springboard to a comprehensive overhaul of governance practices. A cadre of board members worked with the university community to develop a more transparent and engaged style of governing.

Not all crises are self-inflicted. President Scott S. Cowen and the Tulane University board used the destruction caused by Hurricane Katrina as the starting point for strengthening the institution. The devastation catalyzed them to rethink the future of Tulane to make it even stronger and better than in the past.

Performance Warning Signs

Performance measures may not be poetic, but they provide indisputable warning signs that a college or university is headed in the wrong direction. Metrics that cast a backward glance at historical performance, either related to the institution's own standards or to competitors' accomplishments, hold a mirror up to the institution's recent history. If the numbers are clear enough, they can be a powerful inducement for change. Metrics converted to trend lines illuminate the future. Forecasts can trigger action from high-functioning board members who make a habit of scanning the horizon for changes in their institution's competitive environment.

Changes in state financial-aid policy, which made Hendrix College more expensive for its students, led the board to analyze enrollment trends into the future. This intelligence prompted board action before the college experienced enrollment declines. Northern Kentucky University had been overenrolled and underfunded compared with other regional public universities in the state. Projecting current trends in state support into the future revealed that the current business model could not be sustained. Instead of relying on short-term solutions like reducing or freezing expenditures, the president and the board chose to engage in deep budget and operational restructuring.

Benchmarking—comparing an institution's past performance with that of its peers—can indicate that change is due or, more likely, overdue. A pervasive decline in brand appeal over a number of years, evidenced by difficulties in attracting top students, led to change at Oberlin College. Drops in student retention and graduation rates are another clear signal that change is needed. Until recently, colleges and universities guarded those statistics carefully. Now, at least first-level comparisons are widely available. The Education Trust's College Results Online Web site provides accessible data comparing retention, graduation, and transfer rates from peer institutions over time. Users can also construct their own comparison groups.

Other signs of incipient decline, which are slightly less obvious but no less dangerous, include rising tuition discount rates reflecting a drop in attractiveness to students, increases in deferred maintenance, and adverse ratios of debt to income that raise the risk that the institution will fail to meet its debt obligations. The story is bad enough when such indicators are linked to the institution's own past performance. But when competing institutions realize more net revenue from tuition, improve the physical attractiveness of their campuses, and meet their debt obligations easily, the narrative becomes darker and the need for change more compelling.

The University of Dubuque found itself on the wrong side of this divide between haves and have-nots. The negative indicators motivated the board and its new president to spark one of the most dramatic small-university turnarounds in the country as they led a program that tripled enrollment, magnified the endowment, and virtually rebuilt the campus.

Setting High Aspirations to Change

Immediate crises, early warning signs of problems to come, and forecasts of a dire future spur the most action by boards and presidents. But the simple belief that "We can do better"—without a crisis—also motivates exceptional boards to act. A visionary board chair will lead fellow board members, and the institution as a whole, to their next level of excellence.

Board Chair Erna Hoover inspired Trenton State College to begin the trek to excellence that led to the creation of The College of New Jersey. The board chair of the University of North Florida, R. Bruce Taylor, and his partner in change, President John A. Delaney, instigated that institution's more recent aspiration to achieve a reputation for regional service at a national level of quality, akin to the repute of Ohio's Miami University. The board at Northwestern Health Sciences University determined to become "the university of choice in natural health care" by implementing an integrated curricular model. While the vision at this stage remains an aspiration, not an achievement, it continues to guide board-president discussions and remains a genuine goal for the university.

Figure 2.1 Inducement to Change

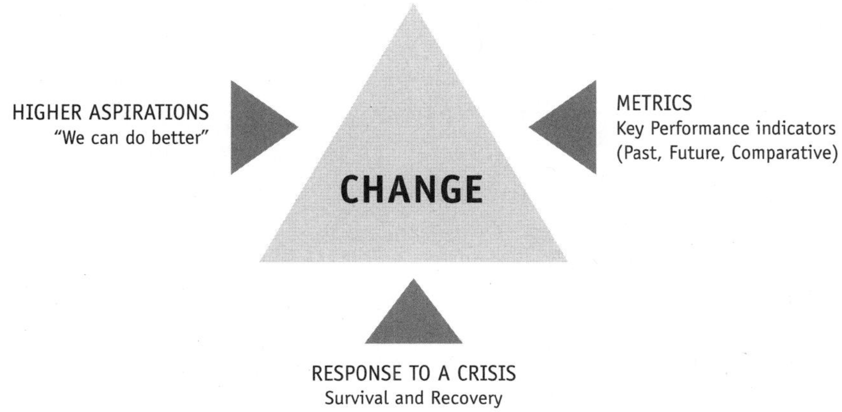

Figure showing a triangle labeled CHANGE in the center, with three arrows pointing toward it:
- HIGHER ASPIRATIONS "We can do better" (left)
- METRICS Key Performance indicators (Past, Future, Comparative) (right)
- RESPONSE TO A CRISIS Survival and Recovery (bottom)

Understanding the Depth of Change Required

Shooting in haste, in bad light, or before identifying the target is dangerous, as every experienced hunter knows. When board members appreciate the depth and kind of change a college or university needs, they will see the target clearly, appreciate the change work before them, and decide if they should play a narrow role or a major one. The news headline, information, or event that motivates the board to act may be only the tip of the iceberg when it comes to understanding the depth of change needed. For example, if enrollment declines are the consequence of staff turnover among admissions recruiters, better management or more training for recruiters may be the fix. But if the problem is deeper, and a college's value proposition no longer meets the demands of the market, the solution requires better understanding of how students view the institution in comparison with its competition.

The board at American University came to appreciate the challenge of identifying the depth of change needed as they realized that excessive executive pay was not primarily the president's problem, but the result of the board's own inattention and chronic lapses in internal communication. As one board member put it, they realized that it was not "Ladner's problem" (referring to the former president, Benjamin Ladner); it was a "governance problem." Part of the change process at American involved a board-led overhaul of governance structures and processes. When Oberlin's board found that that many competitive prospective students were choosing rival institutions, they discovered that the problem was misperception of the college's distinctive benefits. To regain market share, Oberlin needed to rethink the quality of its overall experience as well as the public's perception of that quality. The board initiated, and the college engaged in, an institution-wide effort to revitalize all major functions, including academic offerings, marketing, and fund raising.

Types of Change

*I have a very, very long time horizon. In higher education, you can't
get there in one step. You have to be sensitive to one step at a time.
The academy has a lot of fear of change. Our biggest challenge was to
help people become comfortable with change, that we could make
important changes without changing the soul of the place. It's still Oberlin. One of
our goals was to build that level of confidence.*

—ROBERT S. LEMLE, Chair, Oberlin College

Some change is straightforward, with solutions readily available in the change
repertoire. Other change involves a complex transformation that requires members of
the college community to rethink the institution's mission and their role in it. In the
relatively non-authoritarian world of the academy, where tradition and tenure insulate
faculty from administrative demands, how professors (and to a lesser degree students
and staff members) feel about change often becomes a crucial factor in the success
of a change initiative. Ronald A. Heifetz and Timothy R. Clark, leading thinkers on
change, draw attention to the power of emotional response as distinguished from
logical thinking about change. They contend that managing emotional reactions is as
important as developing logical rationales for a different way of operating, especially if
change requires the community to adapt to uncomfortable new realities.

In his influential taxonomy of change, *Leadership Without Easy Answers* (Harvard
University Press, 1998), Heifetz—like Clark in *Epic Change* (Jossey-Bass, 2007)—
captures the dilemma board members face when confronted with complex challenges
for which the right solutions are ambiguous and may require painful dislocations.
Addressing this dilemma usually requires letting go of familiar values and ways of
operating. The abandonment of once-meaningful, now-dysfunctional attitudes and
beliefs is a tough process, especially in colleges and universities where tradition is
valued.

Heifetz and Clark describe three types of change: operational (Type I), behavioral
(Type II), and adaptive or cultural (Type III) (Figure 2.2). Each type is evident in the
change processes and narratives of colleges and universities.

Figure 2.2 Types of Change

TYPE	CHARACTERISTICS	EXAMPLES
I Operational	Familiar problem Familiar solutions	Refinancing institutional debt Constructing a new science building
II Behavioral	May be involuntary Requires some new learning	Installing a new information system Implementing a new collective bargaining agreement Going to Division I athletics Moving the campus to a new location Adding major online degree programs Expanding student diversity (e.g., recruiting and admitting more international or urban minority students)
III Adaptive or cultural	Strongly felt problem No current solution seems to fit No familiar or comfortable solution Requires individuals to adapt their values, thinking, and behavior to a new reality All alternatives lead to emotional pain Creates some winners, but lots of losers Causes disequilibrium in the community	Admitting men or women to a previously single-gender institution Changing the business model to make each unit responsible for increasing its enrollment Making substantial reductions in the workforce and programs

Type I: Operational Change

Type I change involves familiar problems with solutions that can be plucked from a conventional repertoire. Refinancing debt or constructing a building are complicated changes that require skill and experience, but they are both well within the grasp of most institutions. Boards usually play a well-defined role in these sizeable operational changes. A facilities committee might discuss the selection of an architect, review scale models, and consider the location of a new building. A finance committee that enjoys the board's trust will probably delve into the financial consequences of debt restructuring and report its recommendations to the full board. If board decisions about the building generate controversy—especially if board members are lobbied to support a particular option—board leaders should use their influence to steer the group back to discussions of institutional strategy and out of debates about where to locate the new building.

Type II: Behavioral Change

Type II change triggers community resistance, which can include trenchant opposition, longer-than-predicted implementation schedules, and great expense before the change is finally adopted. Installing an enterprise-wide information system, for example, may seem like a straightforward exercise in changing technologies. But the difficult experience of many institutions attests that it demands comfort with the unfamiliar, far-reaching adaptations in employees' behavior, and armies of consultants to make the change happen. Cost overruns are the norm, not the exception, meaning less money for academic programs, student services, or other institutional activities.

When the costs of a change process are high, when the task is complex both technically and in human terms, and when the terrain is somewhat unfamiliar, boards need to be especially vigilant in asking tough questions and determining that the staff is up to the challenge. Board members who have experience with information technology in larger organizations will be familiar with the technical and human sides of the equation. They can be invaluable to the board in monitoring these systems on its behalf. Leaving the change entirely to the staff is often a mistake in a Type II situation.

Type III: Adaptive or Cultural Change

Type III change is the most complex of all because the problems have no technical solutions. Instead, the college community—board, faculty, staff, and students—must come to terms with the gap between comfortable internal habits and a changed external reality. Heifetz labels these situations adaptive because the leadership task is to help the community adapt to conventional ways of thinking about a new, unfamiliar, and unattractive reality.

While operational change occurs within an institution and behavioral change is connected to an enterprise, adaptive or cultural change is transformation of a college or university. Examples include merging two independent institutions, a for-profit company acquiring a liberal arts college, closing a campus and laying off faculty and staff, and integrating male students into a former women's college. These Type III changes all involve major social and emotional adaptations.

The board's role in adaptive or cultural change is significantly more active for several reasons. Type III change that threatens to destabilize the academic community elicits more controversy, pushback, and public debate than simpler Type I and Type II situations. More faculty no-confidence votes occur in these change situations than in the others. The board needs to be prepared to take the heat and support its president without becoming publically embroiled in the debate. If the controversy on the campus attracts news-media attention, the focus will be on the conflict, not on the complicated issues. The board should be ready to handle the news-media interest, along with the damage to the institution's reputation that may result.

The process of Type III change, because it involves painful dislocations, university politics, and often public participation, is much more complicated than the process of less-radical types of change. The full talent of the board—especially members with experience in the human side of change in complex business, government, and nonprofit enterprises—must be focused on both the immediate drama and the longer-term goals of change.

> *Social sector leaders are not less decisive than business leaders as a general rule; they only appear that way to those who fail to grasp the complex governance and diffuse power structures common to social sectors....[They face] a governance and power structure that render[s] executive-style leadership impractical.*
> — JIM COLLINS *Good to Great and the Social Sectors* (HarperCollins, 2005)

Figure 2.3: Questions to Ask before Engaging in Major Change

Launching major change, especially Type III change, requires sustained board attention from the start. Simply turning the process over to the president, however talented he or she might be, is not enough. Successful board engagement in change leadership begins with careful thought and discussion about the appropriate board role to meet the demands of the situation. The board and the president should discuss six key questions before beginning a change process:

1. Is the problem operational? Does a solution exist within the repertoire of the institution's talent and tools?

2. Is the problem behavioral? Are the right people in place but not doing the right things—or doing the wrong things—to address the issue?

3. Is the problem cultural? Does the whole institution need to adapt its values, attitudes, and behaviors to suit a radically changed competitive environment?

4. What roles should the board and the president adopt to lead constructive change?

5. How should the board equip itself to playing a productive role in the change process?

6. Who else can or must contribute to solving the problem? How should the board and president engage with faculty members and their senates or associations, students and their governments, community leaders, policy makers, and the news media?

Barriers to Inducing Change

In institutions that trace their founding back hundreds of years, the barriers to introducing and bringing about change can be daunting, but not insurmountable. The chapters that follow address strategies and practices for engaging in change, but first it is helpful to acknowledge the three main obstacles facing board members and presidents who seek to assert positive leadership: barriers to the board's effectiveness in leading change; universal sources of failure in organizational change; and forms of resistance peculiar to the academy and its culture.

Obstacles to Board Leadership

Wanting change and making it happen are two different things. Virtually every board member has noble intentions of supporting and strengthening the institution by enabling improvement in quality, reputation, and the capacity to serve social needs. But fewer boards have the talent and experience to lead positive change.

Three main obstacles stand in the way of effective board leadership of change:

- Limited board commitment of time and energy;
- Inadequate board talent and experience with complex organizational change; and
- Presidential wariness of an active board and engaged board members.

The goal of this book is to enhance board change leadership—an agenda that one able college president described, only partially in jest, as "a president's worst nightmare." Although many presidents actively seek board members who want to be intimately engaged, even these presidents are as wary of involved board members as they are of inept ones. This caution is not misplaced. But as the examples in this book confirm, adroit board members working in tandem with strong presidents present a formidable change team that transcends the power of either working alone.

Board members lead busy professional and social lives. Some find the time and energy required of change leadership to be more than they wish to invest. Others have the time but lack the experience that real change leadership requires. And some simply are not interested or view it as outside their role as board members. The best of this dutiful group see their responsibilities as preparing for meetings, attending them, offering carefully considered advice and making sound judgments, voting their conscience, and contributing financially. These backbenchers' counsel and support are valuable, but a board dominated by them will not contribute much to positive change.

Recruiting board members with the commitment, experience, and time to contribute to change is obviously a condition of the board's engagement in change. As an Oberlin board member said, "You should have managed a complex enterprise, for-profit or not, if you really want to bring positive change to a college." Beyond executive experience, this level of board participation requires a personal commitment of time and energy. One group of highly involved board members estimated that they averaged 40 hours a month on governance tasks. But leading change also demands experience in change processes, the intelligence to recognize situations where board leadership contributes to effective change and where it detracts, and the emotional sensitivity to interact appropriately with other players. Board members who are embarking on institutional change should simultaneously adopt a development program to enhance their skills in change leadership (see Chapter 6).

Why Transformation Efforts Fail

John P. Kotter, a professor at Harvard Business School and influential thinker about leading change in the corporation, pinpoints the flaws that cause transformation efforts to fail after leaders have determined change is necessary. Kotter's list applies equally well to colleges and universities:

- Not establishing a great enough sense of urgency;
- Not creating a powerful enough guiding coalition;
- Lacking a vision;
- Under-communicating the vision by a factor of 10;
- Not removing obstacles to the new vision;
- Not systematically planning for and creating short-term wins;
- Declaring victory too soon; and
- Not anchoring changes in the institution's culture.

Misfires also occur before a change initiative is launched. Expanding on Kotter's list, these flaws can be seen in the higher-education context:

- ***Failure to engage the president fully as the pivotal leader.*** When the board initiates change, as it clearly did at Oberlin, Hendrix, Agnes Scott, Northwestern Health Sciences University, and others in the AGB study, the president must become equally enthused and a partner in the leadership of change. That attitude comes most easily to a new president who is hired precisely because the board believes he or she embraces a change agenda. Northwestern Health Sciences University looked within the board for a new president partly because he had participated in the deliberations that led to the board adopting a more-comprehensive mission for the institution. It may take more time and serious conversations to persuade a current president to see change leadership as a major part of the job description. Going through the motions of leading change to placate a board spells doom for a successful board-executive relationship. The agreement of Robert S. Lemle, the Oberlin board's vice-chair (and later chair) to co-chair a strategic planning committee with the current president represents one positive way to make the partnership work.

- ***Mistaking the cure for a crisis as the cure for the underlying problem.*** One board chair described a college as inhabiting a "culture of crisis" that caused it to lurch from one near-catastrophe to another. An enrollment shortfall predicted in the summer led to an "all hands on deck" phone campaign to persuade applicants to attend in the fall. A drop in revenue prompted frantic appeals to donors to bail out the beleaguered institution once again. These short-term measures did not resolve the deeper problem: The college lacked the strong brand appeal and programs that would support it. Only when new board leadership stepped back to articulate what would make the place compelling to prospective students did a much-needed turnaround begin.

- **Unrealistic aspirations for the outcomes of change.** When asked what kind of institution a regional public university should aspire to become, one board member replied that Princeton University represented a worthwhile goal. Ignoring mission, location, and traditions in favor of an unattainable goal adds nothing to the credibility of change. Articulating an aspiration that requires creativity and hard work but is achievable in time for participants to experience the results makes more sense. The board of the University of North Florida embraced an inspiring but practical goal when it endorsed the vision of providing service to its region at "a national level of quality."

- **A disconnect among aspirations, strategies, and resources.** Failure to align the goals of change with the strategies to achieve them and the money to make change happen is probably the most common error in change leadership. Crucial to Oberlin's success in restoring its competitiveness was the board's decision to create a financial model and plan specifically linked to its new strategic objectives.

Resistance Endemic to the Academy

Academics can be blind to the irony of recommending changes in society and other organizations while stoutly resisting change in their own teaching behavior, the organizational structure of departments and colleges, budget allocations, governance and decision-making practices, almost anything to do with athletics, and any other change. This reputation for obstinacy is well deserved. This cultural trait also explains why the Roman Catholic Church, the Parliament of Iceland, and the university are the only three institutions that have existed continuously since the Middle Ages. Academic tradition is a great force for stability, just as it represents a bulwark against the tides of change. Three features of the academy insulate it from change, especially change perceived as imposed by a board, administrators, or outside agencies: the decentralized nature of authority, the tenure system, and the culture of skepticism.

Authority is dispersed throughout a college or university, with each department and school more responsive to the norms of its own discipline than the wishes of an administrator or the board. Political consequences flow from the decentralized model. Members of faculty senates, which typically represent the faculty's voice on academic matters and sometimes most other issues as well, are elected by their departmental peers. The senator's job is to represent the department's interests and protect it from harm. A change that threatens the department, its faculty complement, budget, or ability to maintain a student base will meet stiff resistance.

The tenure system reinforces faculty independence from board and administrative authority. Once a faculty member achieves tenured status, usually after a probationary period of six or seven years, it becomes virtually impossible to dismiss the member except for the most egregious misbehavior. Of course, the strongest case in favor of tenure is that it protects academic freedom from intrusion by anyone with a doctrinaire agenda. When unions and collective bargaining exist, especially in the absence of a strong, academically oriented faculty senate, change comes harder.

Faculty members pay dues to their association to protect their jobs, compensation, and other interests. When bringing change to a unionized institution, change leaders must make the case to union leaders that change is ultimately good for their members. It is essential to secure their acquiescence, if not their outright support. But when change requires adapting to unpleasant but inescapable realities like reduced funding and a less comfortable future, union leaders must be convinced that change from within, no matter how difficult, is better than change imposed from the outside.

The quality that generates the most consistent resistance to change is the trained skepticism of faculty members. The doctoral dissertation—their rite of passage—often begins with a "state of the studies" in which the writer summarizes existing research in order to debunk or at least criticize the findings. The best teachers are often those who question received opinion and encourage their students to think independently as well.

Involving these intelligent, well-educated thinkers early in the change process has several advantages. On a pragmatic level, professors are more apt to buy into changes that they have a hand in making. If faculty representatives are persuaded that change is inevitable and that change they help to engineer is preferable to that imposed upon them, they will help sell the new order to their colleagues. Bringing faculty to the table early also adds thoughtful scrutiny to the change process and results in better ideas overall.

In an unusual example, the faculty senate at American University brought itself to the table for study and discussions of governance reform following the scandal over the board's lack of control of the president's spending and compensation. The senate appointed an ad hoc committee to review and make recommendations on how the board might function better. They found a receptive audience. Working closely with the board, they developed recommendations—most of which were adopted—calling for more transparency and greater faculty involvement with the board.

Neither the decentralization of authority, nor tenure, nor the culture of skepticism makes change impossible. But failure to find constructive ways to bring faculty to the table usually spells disaster for strategic-level change. One university's attempts to introduce a new strategic plan were largely unsuccessful, in part because the faculty felt change was driven exclusively by the board and a president carrying out the board's orders. After several years of conflict punctuated by no-confidence votes in the president and the board, a new board chair met personally with faculty senate leaders to start the process afresh.

Powerful Change in Three Universities
Northern Kentucky University • Northwestern Health Sciences University • American University

Just about all the key measures point to Northern Kentucky University as a high-performing institution that meets or exceeds the most common benchmarks for comprehensive public universities. Its enrollment growth is nearly double that of other Kentucky publics, but it receives less state support per student than any other public university in the state. From 2000 to 2010, the number of graduates in the STEM fields (science, technology, engineering, and mathematics) more than doubled. Growth over the same period in the number of minority graduates was an astounding 230 percent.

Can this pattern of performance be sustained? The board and the president believe so, but only with an ambitious set of changes in the way NKU does business—with the goal of achieving long-term financial stability with far less state support. The initiatives include shrinking the size of the administration and its costs, increasing student-credit-hour productivity per faculty member, reducing the number of credits required for graduation from 128 to 120, and focusing on academic programs and services for which there is demonstrable market demand and potential for net financial return. Any one of these initiatives could be labeled Type I or operational change. But as a comprehensive package designed to accommodate new state-funding realities and student resistance to tuition increases, they surely verge into the more-complex Type II and Type III changes—particularly those involving teaching styles and loads.

The changes at Northwestern Health Sciences University in Bloomington, Minn., are also worth studying for at least three reasons. First, a highly engaged board, convinced that the integrated health-care model is the future for health-care delivery, has initiated and driven them. Second, the board wants to raise the positive visibility of the institution and position it at the forefront of this trend. And third, while some of the changes appear to be of the modest Type I variety—locating a clinical setting for chiropractic students in a conventional hospital, for example—they have required serious adaptive (Type II and at times Type III) adjustments. This combination of operational and cultural change has progressed more slowly than envisioned, and at least one board member who felt his profession as a chiropractor was threatened by the changes chose to withdraw from the board. But the board and the president have persevered, and the university remains convinced that there is no going back to the familiar, comfortable model.

American University experienced complex change of the adaptive or Type III variety. The crisis over board oversight, as well as the negative national publicity generated by the Congressional hearings, provided energy for board members and academic stakeholders, especially faculty members, to engage in a process that went far beyond fixing a compensation problem. Not all board members could live with the changes. In one remarkable instance, the board chair resigned without notice a day before a board meeting. Board leaders, with useful assistance from a faculty senate committee, determined that the best remedy was transparency, inclusiveness, and open communications. By most accounts, they have created a model for board governance that is well worth imitating.

(See Appendix for an overview of the change at these institutions.)

Lessons from Attempts to Lead Change

Prepare for the reality that not all board members will buy into the change.

Change isn't easy, but institutions that work through tough decisions come out stronger. Although some board members resigned at American and Northwestern Health, both boards emerged stronger—with a commitment to transparency in governance and, at Northwestern, a more market-oriented mission for the university.

Appreciate the kind and depth of change required.

Nothing is more dangerous and difficult, Machiavelli said, than attempting to bring a new order to things. The staying power of the familiar and the dubious comfort of the status quo are not to be underestimated. What may look like relatively straightforward Type I or operational change to board members who will remain unaffected by it may appear more complicated and troublesome to those with a personal stake in the status quo. Expect debate, sometimes anger, and occasional resignations. If some board members object, campus employees whose lives will be changed, as well as alumni and others with an emotional stake in the past, are likely to object as well. A board and president prepared for criticism and opposition will be better able to cope with it than those who naively believe change comes easily.

Recognize the trenchant aversion to change that often exists in the academy.

If constructively involved in the change process, faculty members will usually contribute thoughtfully and eventually support the outcome. If left out of the debate or if they feel they receive only pro forma attention, they will likely resist the change and criticize the would-be change leaders.

Acknowledge that change requires a strong partnership between the board and the president.

At American, the new president and the board took governance reform and rebuilding the board/campus-community relationship as a joint responsibility. A new strategic plan represented the capstone work. Change at Northern Kentucky arose from the board's and the president's commitment to avoid temporary measures in favor of enterprise-wide change that would position the university for a future far less reliant on state subsidy. When pushback comes as a consequence of adjusting workloads and criteria for program review and approval, the board and the president will operate as a united front. At Northwestern Health Sciences, the board and the president regularly discuss, and sometimes debate, who is responsible for which aspects of implementing the new integrated health mission. But no daylight shines between them when it comes to their joint commitment to making this model of professional health-care preparation the core of the curriculum.

Topics for Board and President Discussion

1. ***Reasons for change.*** Why are we contemplating change? If we face a crisis, do we understand its deeper causes as well as its immediate manifestation?

2. ***Trends and forecasts.*** What do our metrics tell us about the school's performance when compared with our peers? What does tracing current trends into the future tell us about our competitive position?

3. ***Types of change.*** What changes should we consider? Are they fairly straightforward, and does the current staff have the experience to conduct them? Or are they more complex, requiring additional thought and maybe some outside help? What can we learn from institutions that have faced similar challenges and met them successfully?

4. ***Adaptive change.*** Are we facing radical change that will require serious adaptations in the way faculty members teach and students learn, in the way the institution is organized, or in the pattern of allocating resources? Whatever the type of change, how can we prepare ourselves to lead it?

5. ***Stakeholder involvement.*** What groups do we need to involve in the change process, and how can we best engage them? Should we leave all of this up to the president, or should the board become involved with faculty and staff members, students, and others? What forms could this involvement take?

Chapter 3

THE BOARD AND THE PRESIDENT: THE ESSENTIAL RELATIONSHIP

The working relationship between the president and the board is the essential alliance in bringing about positive change. A talented president linked to an acquiescent board can get some good things done. In partnership with an able, more active group of board members, still more is possible. But fundamental change is nearly impossible if the board is simply interested and agreeable. No sports team wins year after year with only one great player. The same holds true for governance teams at colleges and universities. As one experienced board member puts it, "We need each other to get anything done."

Effective teamwork in pursuit of change requires finely tuned balance and coordination among the talents and capabilities of board members and president. A proactive and concerned board yoked to a change-averse president can do little except perhaps bring improvement to its own processes—and find a new president. Conversely, when a diffident board in a climate that demands change reins in the potential of a capable president, it risks losing a good leader and leaving the institution in limbo, or worse.

Board members should be wary of assuming that change in the academy comes as quickly as it can in organizations where the lines of authority are more clear-cut and the environment is more receptive to change. Presidents seeking change must negotiate complex terrain. The protections of tenure, the tradition of shared governance, rules codified in collective-bargaining agreements, and a culture famously averse to change all work to inhibit bringing about a new order. The good news, however, is that an able board coupled with an equally talented president committed to a change partnership is almost unbeatable. When both honor their respective roles, appreciate that interdependence is essential, and commit to mutual support through all the potential crisis points in the relationship, the president and the board make a formidable change-leadership team.

This chapter addresses these questions on the topic of how boards and presidents aid one another in bringing positive change:

- What does the interdependence of boards and presidents really mean, and how is it demonstrated?
- What are the options for board-president collaboration in change leadership?
- How should boards and presidents together engage with the faculty in bringing about positive change?
- What common mistakes impede the change relationship?
- What critical turning points in the relationship occur during the change process?

Highlighting effective board-president relationships are the stories of change at Oberlin College and Widener University, along with examples from other institutions where this leadership partnership made a vital difference in initiating, planning, and guiding major change agendas.

Interdependence and the Essential Relationship

Grounded in trust, candor, and integrity, the relationship between the board and the president works best when both partners recognize their mutual reliance. "The board and the president together agree that their relationship is interdependent (each contributes to it in the interests of the other) and the relative strength of the relationship creates the presidency," writes Edward Penson.[2] The most-effective partnerships reflect a genuine appreciation for each partner's singular strengths: the board's external vantage point and capacity to focus on the long term, for example, or the president's deep knowledge of the institution and experience in the field of higher education.

Any board member or president who likens the connection as boss to underling will underperform dramatically. To be sure, the board can fire the president, while the president can't do the reverse. But in most relationships, boards and presidents reach agreement from near-equal positions of power. A board that is unable to strike what the president regards as a fair deal will likely get less-than-full commitment in the bargain and may soon be searching for a new partner.

At times, the power rests primarily with the board. The energy for beginning the turnaround at Oberlin College, after the financial difficulties of the early 2000s, came from the board, although the board and then the president quickly became active partners in the change process. Then there are times when the balance shifts to the president. At Widener University, the board knew the institution needed change and a change leader, but the new president, James T. Harris, led in articulating a vision of civic engagement as the dominant strategic direction for the university.

> *We don't always agree with Steve [Jordan, the president] at the start, but we trust him and usually agree to his proposals, provided that there is solid accountability. We know that failure sometimes accompanies risk, but we believe that risk is good.*
> —ADELE PHELAN, Former Chair, Metropolitan State College of Denver

Dimensions of Interdependence

Wise presidents and board members focus on three especially meaningful dimensions of interdependence: conferred authority, shared learning, and collaborative decision making.

----

[2] Edward Penson, *Board and President: Facilitating the Relationship* (Association of State Colleges and Universities, 2003), p. 16.

Conferred Authority

The board and the president confer credibility and thus authority on one another through public and private actions. If either party minimizes in word or deed the authority of the other, the effectiveness of the partnership diminishes. The board confers executive authority on the president through legal actions, public statements, and academic rituals. An employment contract, news-media announcements, a formal inauguration, and continuing public and private acknowledgment of the president by title are all expressions of authority. The president confers authority on the board formally whenever he or she seeks official board approval for a proposed action, and informally in discourse on campus and beyond when referring to the board as the ultimate decision maker. Academic rituals like commencement, when the president awards degrees "by the authority vested in me," reinforce this delegation.

Shared Learning

If knowledge is power, then the mutual sharing of information and insight underpins the wise use of board and executive authority. This educational process flows both ways. The president and his or her staff provide the institutional information that board members need to make enlightened decisions. They educate their partners in leadership with accurate, succinct materials that inform but do not overwhelm—not only as background before board meetings, but also periodically throughout the year. Since most board members hail from nonacademic backgrounds, the president also has a duty to help translate for them the values and mores of academic culture.

For their part, board members can provide useful intelligence about the thinking of the board itself, as well as what's happening outside the academy. Yet board members have no monopoly on intelligence from beyond higher education, and often they are more knowledgeable about institutional values than a new president might be. The key point is that sharing information and intelligence from whatever worlds they are most familiar with is essential to making informed decisions, and it is a hallmark of a mature board-president relationship.

Indeed, although the board is the senior partner, it must allow the president to be its teacher upon occasion. By the same token, the president must become a student of the board to receive its collective wisdom and maintain its support. Often the board is in closer touch with the sentiments of the community, the alumni, and perhaps the legislature, as well as with the college's heritage. A new president, especially one without prior experience at the campus, would do well to learn from board members whose insights are gained from long involvement. For their part, board members should be attentive to the lessons their president offers on the culture of decision making in the academy in general. A president can help the board understand change strategies, such as the transformative power of civic engagement at Widener, that are part of his or her portfolio.

Collaborative Decision Making

Informed decision making is not an event for which responsibility is clearly delineated, but rather a process marked by robust communication between the board and the president that flows before and after executive action occurs. The process is generated from the shared learning and information-gathering described above, and it continues with the analysis, discussion, debate, and deliberation that precede such executive action. Ideally, the circle closes with evaluation of the relative success of the action and lessons learned from the process.

The more consequential the action, the more the board and the president—and a host of players including faculty members, community leaders, and elected officials in the case of public institutions—discuss the options ahead of the action; review progress or lack thereof during implementation; and assess the effects along the way. The board plays an instrumental role at the policy and conceptual levels throughout the change process. Richard Chait and his colleagues describe a "generative curve" in which the opportunity for the board to have a meaningful influence declines as issues become strategic options and plans.[3] Board members' involvement in the early, generative stage promotes genuine engagement in decision making.

An Absolute Prerequisite: Trust and Confidence

The amalgam of thought and emotion expressed in phrases like "I trust you to be honest with me" and "I believe you have the talent to lead this institution" is the essence of any high-functioning relationship, but it is especially important in times of change. Chairman Mao famously avowed that a revolution is not a garden party. The same holds true for institutional change. The relationship will be tested by adversity. There will be critics of the change and its leaders. Some change strategies will fail. Some will be highly unpopular. Economic downturns will dampen enthusiasm and constrain resources. Unanticipated reversals such as athletics scandals, accidents, and catastrophes like Hurricane Katrina will occur. These events will put great stress on the change process and the working partnership between the board and president. Both will need to dip into their reservoir of mutual trust and confidence to persevere together.

The level of interaction between board members and the president, and indeed the entire academic community, varies with the kind of change the institution is experiencing (Figure 3.1). The more the change moves from the largely operational or technical level to the realm where cultural values are at stake, the more the board must be attentive and involved.

---

[3] Richard Chait, William Ryan, and Barbara Taylor, *Governance as Leadership: Reframing the Work of Nonprofit Board* (John Wiley & Sons, 2005).

Figure 3.1 Participation in Change

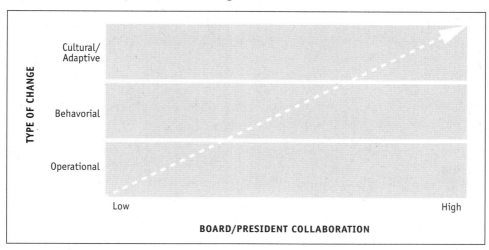

The board and the president need to trust the other's honesty, competence, and devotion to strengthening the institution and fulfilling its mission. This reciprocal trust allows the two to disagree in private sessions without jeopardizing their fundamental relationship. When there are strains, they have the emotional intelligence to heal them. And in the spirit of the common-sense "treaty of no surprises," they always share news, especially bad news, with each other before anyone else.

The alliance also requires a degree of theatricality. Often by prior agreement, if not rehearsal, boards publicly underscore a concern or initiative in order to emphasize their solidarity with the president on the matter. Part of the art of change leadership is calling attention to what needs changing, and the president and the board should use their respective bully pulpits to underscore their top priorities.

A helpful, even necessary, attribute of the board-president relationship is personal support for the president—usually from the chair, and sometimes from another board member or two. A show of solicitude and the availability of a confidant during a particularly stressful phase of the presidency or when the president experiences a personal crisis is not only a decent thing to do, but it also strengthens the partnership. This can work the other way, as the president shows support for board members and board leaders.

The confidant aspect of the relationship works as long as both parties honor the boundaries of their respective positions. Empathetic support for the president does not absolve the board from evaluating his or her performance. Nor can a president expect the board's genuine sympathy to erase the need for continuously earning the board's confidence.

How Boards and Presidents Collaborate

How can presidents and boards interact most effectively as change is contemplated and then put into motion? The best decisions begin with thinking about and discussing the problem, its causes, options for dealing with it, how the options might be carried out, and so on. In this "upstream" stage in the process of change, boards and presidents need the opportunity for learning, questioning, and debate. The most-intense collaboration between boards and presidents appropriately comes in this early stage, where there is more thinking than acting, when they are framing the questions and problems rather than attempting to resolve them.

Collaboration in making change ranges from suggesting a few ideas to collectively arriving at a course of action. These definitions borrow from the thinking of management and leadership experts Ronald A. Heifetz, Victor H. Vroom, and Arthur G. Jago.

1. ***Unilateral action*** occurs when one party or individual makes the call with minimal input from others. Heifetz reminds us, however, that even an autocrat is influenced to some degree by the input of subordinates.

2. ***Consultative processes*** unfold when one party provides information to the other but does not share in making the decision.

3. ***Participatory modes*** of involving groups in change invite more dialogue, and the issues discussed are more wide-ranging than in the consultative model. To participate in change implies a more equal relationship among the parties than in either the unilateral environment or the consultative relationship. Still, one party is the decider, and the other is not.

4. ***Consensual approaches*** mean that both parties discuss all the options and come to a mutually satisfying decision. This mode includes the consultative and participatory types of communication, but it goes further to result in genuine joint decision making.[4]

When Unilateralism Works

Some would argue that the unilateral mode is never justified in the academy, where mutual respect and inclusive decision making are paramount. This argument is usually true, but not always. When a crisis demands quick action or time is of the essence to seize a sudden opportunity, unilateral decision making is necessary. And, of course, the president or chancellor has authority to make unilateral decisions, without board consent, on most administrative and operational matters. But, the problems that arise in higher education almost always allow some time for consultation.

[4] Ron Heifetz, *Leadership Without Easy Answers* (Harvard University Press, 1994), p. 121.

Decisiveness quickly administered by the board is the order of the day when there is an active or incipient scandal involving the president, and he or she has proven to be incompetent or unable to lead for other reasons. Only the board can make this kind of decision. Policing its own members, of course, is the board's province. David W. Oskin, the longtime and highly effective chair at Widener University, could be very direct in working with the nominating committee to tell nonperforming board members at the end of their terms, and sometimes before, that their services would no longer be required.

A complex case arises when the campus has not been able to agree on such controversial mission-centric issues as becoming coeducational or dropping a major sport. The board may say, "We would prefer consensus on this choice, but since there is none, it is our responsibility to decide." The board should not take lightly the choice to make a unilateral decision, in part because it runs the risk of undermining the president's authority and inviting accusations of arbitrary decision making. But when an institution faces an existential challenge and there is no hope for agreement on the hard choices required to preserve itself, then the board must act—even if the decision is highly unpopular in some quarters. The decision to close Tulane for a time following the devastation of Hurricane Katrina was a joint decision between the president and board, as there was precious little time for discussion among the broad campus community.

Consultation before the Choice

Acquiring information from informed sources and listening to their viewpoints—consultation—is a healthy activity as long as it remains clear who holds the power to decide. When a president changes the senior leadership team for any reason—key staff depart or are asked to leave, new skill sets are required to meet higher expectations or pursue new strategies—it is his or her call to make. Because the quality of senior officers is crucial to carrying out major change, the board has a legitimate stake in the choice and a responsibility to express their views. But they should understand from the start that the decision resides with the president. In a parallel instance, the board is responsible for its own organization, bylaws, and the evaluation and occasional discipline of its members. The president's advice, taken in a consultative mode, should be a welcome addition to the board's deliberations.

At Thunderbird, the board is largely credited with making the call to reduce substantially the number of faculty teaching foreign languages after the dramatic plunge in enrollment of international students. The board consulted with the president and others at the school on the impact of its decision. Out of these discussions came the requirement that incoming students possess world-language fluency, a much-less-expensive alternative to preserving one of the school's core features.

At Northwestern Health Sciences University, extensive discussion within the board and the institution preceded the board's decision to pursue an integrated curricular model and to offer clinical experiences in conventional hospital settings. But the dramatic change would not have arisen from campus discussions alone. Only a board convinced that trends in health-care delivery and funding demanded a new approach had the authority to redirect the university's mission.

> *Colleges and universities have a tradition of both academic freedom and constituent participation—commonly called "shared governance"—that is strikingly different from business and more akin to that of other peer-review professions, such as law and medicine.*
>
> —AGB Statement on Board Responsibility for Institutional Governance (AGB, 2010)

Participating in the Debate but Not the Decision

Participation means playing a more active role than just advising, but not so much as to cast a vote in the decision itself. Much shared governance in higher education falls into this category. Widener University's board decided to alter its organizational structure to include a civic-engagement committee with a new board member—a nationally recognized expert on civic engagement—as the chair. The decision involved a high degree of participation by the board and the president, who encouraged the change to align the board's work with the university's strategic direction. As an expert on developing greater civic engagement in a university setting, the president knew the prospective committee chair and his work. Following some deliberation and conversation with the president, the board voted to make the change.

The board of Oberlin College voted in favor of a strategic plan after a process that involved deep participation by the board and the president. The faculty also formally endorsed the plan. The board sought faculty participation in a parallel plan to ensure Oberlin's financial stability, but it did not ask for faculty endorsement. Believing itself to be ultimately responsible for the fiscal health of the institution, the board decided that it would not ask the faculty to endorse a plan that would reduce the size of the tenure-track cadre by cutting a limited number of open positions.

Consensus in the Choice

To cite public-opinion analyst and social scientist Daniel Yankelovich's happy phrase, there is a "magic of dialogue" when those involved develop and agree on better ideas than they held at the beginning. Whether the result of generative thinking (Harvard professor Richard Chait's term) or "thinking out loud," robust, nothing-off-the-table conversations between the president and the board often result in a harmony of ideas—or at least an acceptable compromise—unimagined at the start. While the board may take a formal vote at a subsequent meeting to confirm the outcome of these magic dialogues, the reality is that both parties have come to a substantive meeting of minds during the discussion.

Extensive deliberation and debate among trustees and the president is part of the governance culture at Metropolitan State College of Denver (see Chapter 5). Strategic-level change, whether the proposed faculty "pay-for-performance" compensation model, the addition of master's programs, or the decision to add substantial numbers of full-time faculty, always follows a pattern of intense discussion followed by compromise and eventually consensus that allows Metro State to move forward.

It takes time for the magic of dialogue to work, but absent a life-threatening crisis or emergency that demands immediate action, it is far better to take the time to earn consensus upstream than to face chronic opposition later in the process. It is no coincidence that both Widener and Oberlin took a year and a half to develop and reach agreement on their strategic changes.

Matching Board-President Collaboration to the Type of Change

The extent of board-president collaboration varies depending on whether the change is considered operational, behavioral, or adaptive (See Chapter 2 for a review of these three categories of change.) Operational or technical changes (Type I) that are well within the competence of staff call for little board participation. An exception might be a situation in which one or more board members hold special knowledge that enables them to act as unpaid consultants to the president, as long as this role does not portend conflicts of interest or the misuse of board authority.

When technical issues combine with a high likelihood of that behavioral change will be required (Type II), the problem is trickier. Opening a sizeable new campus or acquiring or starting a new program such as a dental or pharmacy school illustrate complex challenges with daunting technical dimensions in finance, law, planning, and more—along with equally complex and potentially disruptive social change involving faculty and staff. In such processes, the board and the president must communicate regularly about the progress of change and its inevitable problems.

The most complicated type of change—adaptive or Type III change—demands profound adjustments in attitude, values, and behavior on the part of the university community. The need for board-president collaboration intensifies (Figure 3.1). An institutional merger, a shift from a residential to a commuter-based school, or a transformation from a classroom- and lecture-oriented educational model to an online model all may require serious adaptations, depending on the traditions and self-image of the institution. In such scenarios, the board should work closely with the president and the entire academic community.

Large-scale adaptation often includes adjustments to the mission, threats to the brand, and probabilities of conflict on campus. Board members' visible presence and active participation during discussions of change can be reassuring to faculty members, staff members, and students as they work through the conceptual and emotional issues. Listening to the debate will help board members more fully understand the problems as stakeholders perceive them. They will be better able to advise the president and understand the stresses on him or her.

Specific change initiatives require varying degrees of board-president collaboration (Figure 3.2). The visioning phase that usually precedes concrete planning involves high levels of interaction by both parties. The board would be less involved in hiring new staff to carry out the plan but more focused on board structure and leadership—with input but not high participation in the decision by the president. Projects in the lower left quadrant—such as a curriculum change or a new management information system—require less presidential and board attention.

Figure 3.2 President and Board Collaboration in Decision Making

	GOOD GOVERNANCE	**STRATEGIC LEADERSHIP**
HIGH	• Elect new board chair • Restructure board committees	• Problem analysis • Visioning process • Strategic financial plan • Strategic planning • Major decision
	PRESIDENTIAL DELEGATION	**PRESIDENTIAL MANAGEMENT**
LOW	• Major building construction • Curriculum change • Revised information management system	• Hire new senior staff • Change academic calendar

Board Involvement in Decisions

LOW — President Involvement in Decisions — HIGH

Involving the Faculty

While the relationship between the board and the president is the foundation for successful change, it is essential to engage the faculty in serious dialogue when the change involves fundamental issues like mission, strategic direction, curriculum, programs, or various aspects of the teaching-learning model. When it comes to genuinely improving academic programs, making the student learning experience richer and more challenging, and redesigning the curriculum, there is simply no way to do it without the teaching faculty.

Creating the Odyssey program as a signature educational offering at Hendrix College to engage students in global, artistic, and other pursuits, or developing civic engagement as a major part of the Widener ethos, coud not have occurred without faculty participation and support. To be sure, involving other stakeholders—including students, staff members, alumni, donors, neighbors, opinion leaders, and elected officials—almost always makes sense. But faculty engagement is especially crucial—and often complicated for boards and board members unfamiliar with the traditions of shared governance.

Faculty Engagement in Practice

AGB's 2010 statement on shared governance is intended to present a balanced and realistic definition of the range and limits of faculty prerogatives by emphasizing their vital importance in decisions in curriculum and pedagogy. The reality is that substantive change will come about only if faculty members—those already tenured or on track to receive tenure—are deeply engaged in the process. In addition to the force of tradition, there are at least two practical reasons for this.

First, faculty members are the experts when it comes to education and research. It would be foolish to suppose that a board and president, however experienced or intelligent, could substitute their knowledge of an academic subject or academic standards for those of a group of teachers and researchers. A hospital board would no more suggest changing procedures in an operating room without the concurrence of the surgeons than a college or university board should propose changing the educational process without faculty participation and agreement.

The second reason to involve the faculty members is their stature as a political force to be recognized within the institution. This power may be formalized in a union contract or in board-approved faculty senate bylaws. Involving faculty members in discussions of major change and requesting their explicit endorsement leads to more harmonious working relationships.

Restoring Oberlin's competitive edge and supporting Widener's shifting emphasis to civic engagement came about through intense conversations among faculty and board members. There were contentious moments at both institutions when board commitment to change was tested, but in both cases the faculty gave its overwhelming endorsement. At Oberlin, the faculty vote on the change agenda was an astonishing 170 to 33 (with two abstentions). At Widener, an exceptional number of faculty and staff members now rank the university as a "best college to work for," according to a survey by the *Chronicle of Higher Education.*

The change agenda at American University required a dramatic makeover of the way the board did business. Usually, changes in board processes remain the province of the board, perhaps with suggestions from the president. At American, however, given that it was lapses in board oversight that led to the scandal over the president's compensation and threats of Congressional intervention, the board welcomed faculty input partly to symbolize a new era of open governance. In parallel with the board's own review of its processes, a faculty committee examined governance at the board level and offered its recommendations for reform. The board adopted many of the suggestions.

Vehicles for Including Faculty Members in Change

The most-effective ways for presidents and boards to include the faculty in a change process are to forge a positive relationship before the need for change and then to engage them in defining and carrying out change when it is needed. Ideas for sustaining effective working relationships and giving the faculty a voice include:

- Faculty membership on the board;
- Faculty membership on board committees;
- Regular time on the board's agenda for faculty presentations on academic programs and issues; and
- Opportunity for social interaction around board meetings and on other occasions.

It should be noted that not all governance experts think it is wise to have faculty members actually sit on the board; they prefer to keep the various lines of authority—the board, the faculty senate, and president's cabinet—clean and clear. But once an obvious need for change is identified, there are multiple opportunities to involve faculty. The board can:

- Form joint board-faculty task forces, sometimes co-chaired by a faculty member and a board member, to demonstrate the board's commitment to sharing the work of change;
- Hold well-structured meetings for discussing the broad directions for change with large groups of faculty members. Use a group-process technique, such as Open Space Technology, that is designed to help groups reach consensus on large strategic questions;
- Give visible board attention to faculty contributions, especially during board meetings, as a way of confirming board respect for faculty involvement; and
- Seek formal endorsement of the change from the faculty senate or equivalent body. Do so only when appropriate and when the outcome can be safely predicted.

Repairing a Damaged Relationship with Faculty

What if relationships between board, president, and faculty during a period of dramatic change have been contentious or worse? If the institution enjoys the luxury of time, devoting some months or more to restoring trust is a logical first step. When time is in short supply, a "shared commitments" conversation can jumpstart a more productive working relationship marked by open-mindedness, collegiality, and collaboration.

Some of these conversations begin in difficult circumstances. Dissatisfied faculty at Agnes Scott College got the board's attention with a no-confidence vote in the president. As the board introduced change to the college and to its own structure and processes, the tense board-faculty relationship received much-needed attention. Several conversations, some strained, between faculty and board members eventually yielded a meeting of minds, as both sides found common ground in their shared goal of strengthening Agnes Scott. Over time, a much more open and productive relationship between the faculty and the board developed.

A Caution

Although open communication among faculty members, president, and board will yield better ideas and greater faculty support for change, it will also probably lead to attempted lobbying for special causes, programs, and policies. This special pleading can be helpful. At Thunderbird School of Global Management, faculty members' concerns over reductions in their ranks alerted the board to a brewing conflict, enabling it to mediate the dispute before it seriously interrupted the change required to restore financial balance. But boards need to recognize when faculty members or others are simply making the case for their own interests. The motto of "no daylight between the board and the president" in public needs to be rigorously applied.

Impediments to Partnership

Flaws in the relationship between the board and the president—which usually involve either exaggerating or minimizing the other party's potential to contribute—can trump their mutual intent to make things better. There are plenty of ways to fail at making change, including some of the following board errors and presidential misfires.

Board Errors

Mandating Change on the Unwilling or Unable

Foisting a change agenda on a president who can't or won't carry it out or who is not persuaded that the change is right for the times is a recipe for frustration. At a large state university, board members dissatisfied with the lack of direction imposed a mandate on the president to begin a strategic planning initiative that he was poorly equipped to lead. No-confidence votes, bad press, and strained relations all the way around were the chief outcomes. The lesson is that simply ordering change does not make it happen.

Riding the Board Hobby-Horse

It is a mistake as well for board members to take on some aspect of change by themselves. At a healthy but relatively obscure liberal arts college, a new board chair and several of his friends on the board decided, without benefit of conversation with the president, to lead a branding effort on behalf of the college. As in so many smaller institutions that lack national or even regional prominence, this cabal felt that their college was the "best kept secret" in the country. Fortunately, when the group broached the idea to the full board, the wisdom of the majority prevailed. The whole board endorsed a more integrated approach to marketing, with the president firmly in charge.

Change at Oberlin and Widener was grounded in the genius of the institution, not in the idiosyncratic interests of a group of board members or anyone else. Oberlin's chair, Robert Lemle, expressed this spirit: "We needed to develop confidence that we could change and still be Oberlin." A Widener board member said that while college rankings were not ignored, it was much more important to "run their own race" in defining strategic directions. That race led to national recognition for Widener's high level of civic engagement.

Disengaging from the Change Process

The other extreme is equally problematic. Even an adroit president can't successfully lead robust change without visible and active board engagement. Change in the academy works best when board members demonstrate in word and deed that the process is important to them and the institution. The change process presents several opportunities for the board to display its commitment to change, the plan to bring it about, and the role of their president in leading it.

Presidential Misfires

Minimizing the Board's Potential

Some presidents still see the board more as a problem to be managed rather than a collaborator to be trusted. Isolating the board guarantees disengaged board members, early departure of able people, lackluster support when the inevitable pushback occurs, and fewer good ideas in the mix. Engaging the board in the quintessential responsibilities—setting strategic direction, ensuring long-term financial analysis and planning, fund raising, and the like—requires presidential activism if the board historically has been passive in these areas. Moving boards to a high-functioning level has the added benefit of increasing their commitment to the institution when it comes to advocacy and raising money. When change involves topics well within the realm of competence of many board members—for example, strategic finance, marketing and branding, or real-estate acquisition and development—it is shortsighted not to take advantage of this experience.

Granting too Much Authority to the Board

"I work for the board," lamented one beleaguered president when faced with faculty opposition to a board-inspired initiative. Academic communities prefer that their presidents put the institution's welfare ahead of what many will see as secondary priorities of the board. A president who appears beholden to the board will jeopardize the implicit vote of confidence from academics that is necessary to lead. In addition, if the board comes to believe that the president exists to do its bidding, the change partnership is replaced by an autocratic and poorly informed group at the helm.

Turning Points in the Relationship

At inevitable moments in the board-president relationship, it becomes deeper and more effective or remains superficial and less successful than it might be. Whether the board and the president realize the potential for a closer working relationship depends on their honesty and courage. One willing partner is not enough. Failure to overcome the obstacles may not be immediately apparent. As time passes, however, the full potential for positive change will remain elusive because only one party, or perhaps neither, is really committed to the change partnership.

Every interpersonal relationship experiences analogous turning points when rapport becomes more intimate or the parties fail to capture that potential. In the board-president relationship, the critical points are:

- Initial agreement to work together to bring positive change;
- Joint commitment to a plan of action;
- Expression of unqualified support in the face of pushback from the faculty and external groups;
- Steps to restore trust and respect in the relationship after a strain; and
- Endgame that anticipates the close of the liaison.

Initial Agreement to Change

The pledge to work together to advance the institution typically emerges during the hiring process and continues as the candidate becomes the president. During the interview, both parties check each other out. The would-be president asks: What are they really seeking? Do I concur that is what the place needs? Can I deliver and am I willing to try? The board wants to know: Does she really understand the problems? Does she have the talent and courage to address them? Can we work together? If the answers are positive, the two sides usually strike a deal. Ideally, both explicitly commit to a change partnership that will endure throughout the presidency.

Widener University's hiring of a new president illustrates a successful initial agreement. The person who was ultimately selected had sized up Widener's malaise fairly quickly. He told the board, in effect, "If you want someone to build an engaged university that is committed to working with the neighboring community and builds an ethic of positive action into the curriculum, I'm your man. If you don't want this kind of change, you should pick someone else." He and the board came to a meeting of the minds on this point.

Oberlin College had two presidents during the change process, and therefore two stages of initial agreement. The first agreement occurred when the president and the board vice-chair agreed to co-chair a planning effort. After that president's resignation later in the change process, the hiring of a new leader represented another contract in the change partnership.

While the agent of change is most frequently a new president, as the Oberlin case illustrates, a sitting president may team with the board to redirect the institution, or a senior officer at the institution may assume the presidency. In both instances, the president and the board would do well to act as if they were making a fresh start in identifying the institution's needs and determining the kind of change required to remediate its problems.

Commitment to a Plan

Among the lessons from Widener and Oberlin is that change requires a concrete plan complete with secondary objectives, measures, location of responsibility, a schedule, and strong links to the budget. That plan can take significant time to create. At Widener, the entire process, from visioning to community dialogues to the final draft, consumed 18 months. Oberlin's planning process took about the same amount of time, from inception to faculty and board endorsement. Both boards view planning not as a periodic ritual largely devoid of impact, but as the practical roadmap that enables the institution to reach a new destination. For both, the strategic plan forms the backbone of the boards' work.

Failure to develop a meaningful plan or commit to it is a common experience. In a dynamic environment where threats and opportunities abound, the looser approach is a seductive alternative. This opportunistic model—with vague connections among the plan, the budget, and indicators of progress—brings with it the temptation to substitute anecdotal success stories for real achievement. An unrealistic plan, representing dreams more than possibilities, is a fantasy and not a plan at all. Making periodic adjustments to the plan—keeping it "evergreen," as a Widener board member put it—helps ensure that it will remain meaningful. Failure to do so renders the plan obsolete fairly quickly.

Unqualified Support in the Face of Pushback

Change and resistance are inevitable partners. Virtually every significant change process described in this book met opposition from the forces of the status quo, a group with a different vision, people displaced from power, or those who simply didn't like the change leaders or their direction. Often this opposition comes as a delegation from the faculty to the board seeking a change of leadership, direction, or both. It may take the form of actual or threatened votes of no confidence. If change threatens cherished memories or values, the challenge may come from alumni, boosters, and longtime friends of the institution. The criticism may be soft-spoken or raucous, focused on a single objectionable issue or as wide-ranging as an antipersonnel land mine, reported in the news media or conducted through clandestine back channels. But it is inevitable.

Unqualified support in the same channel as the opposition is required. A delegation of professors with a host of motives met with the Widener board to protest the new president's initiatives, alleging that he had lost the support of the faculty. In response, the vice-chair asserted that the president had the support of the board. An anonymous survey of hundreds of Widener faculty and staff members, conducted by the *Chronicle of Higher Education* a few years after this event, reported overwhelming support for the administration and the university's strategic directions.

Oberlin's board remained resolute in the face of criticism of the plan and the president from some disgruntled professors. Members of this unhappy group encouraged their students to poll for a no-confidence vote in the president and petitioned for her ouster, while advancing an alternative plan. The large majority of faculty members ultimately endorsed the original plan—an outcome that may not have occurred had the board blinked in the face of pushback from a small group.

Providing unqualified support doesn't mean ignoring what critics have to say or refusing to learn from the opposition. The board can give the president a quiet bit of advice to be more attentive to a group or issue, to shore up support with those favoring the change, or to spend more time making the case for doing things differently. When the chips are down, however, the board must express as publicly as appropriate its fundamental support for the president and the change agenda. Usually, this endorsement will quell at least the outward expression of pushback.

Restoring Strained Relationships

The good of the institution sometimes demands action from the board or president that offends the other party. Firing or not hiring a locally popular figure may be one example. Edward Penson, an experienced president and student of the presidency, points out that a vital talent for anyone in this position is "the ability to establish strong relationships quickly and well." An able president, Penson says, must also be able to occasionally "strain that relationship for the good of the institution, and then reforge it for the good of the institution." [5]

Leaders at Oberlin and Widener reported no serious strains between the president and the board. They attributed this harmony to factors mentioned here: profound agreement on strategic goals, commitment to a specific plan of action, unflagging board support in the face of opposition, and regular communication between the president and board members.

Preparing the Final Act for a New Opening

Succession planning, which heralds the end of one relationship and the beginning of another, is honored more in word than in deed. The president's eventual departure and replacement is an occasional topic for discussion between a long-serving president and the board. But that conversation focuses less on who comes next and more on the special opportunity for change leadership that comes with the endgame. "If we were starting over at this university with what we know now, what would we do?" is a fruitful question that animates board discussions at academic institutions.

To be sure, the closing of a successful presidency is a time to honor the incumbent's achievements. But those last years present an opportunity for making tough choices that might daunt a new leader, especially if it is widely known that the final phase has begun. Closing a program that is no longer relevant, securing retirement dates from unproductive senior staff (or firing them), and making tough budget decisions are all choices that a late-stage president can make with near impunity. Difficult choices, taken with board support, will leave the institution positioned for a better future under new leadership. Former president Nancy S. Dye's legacy at Oberlin will be her work with the board and faculty in developing positive change strategies.

----

[5] Penson, *Board and President*, p. 12.

Figure 3.3 brings together two major themes of this book: the importance of the board-president partnership in leading change and the building of a stronger institution over time. Leaving aside for the moment the intrusion of external change inhibitors, as well as the occasional accelerants, this illustration links the inevitable turning points to institutional progress. College and university lives are not as smooth as this curve suggests. But there are few exceptions to the rule that close board-president relationships contribute mightily to institutional strength.

Figure 3.3 Milestones in the Change Trajectory

	Mutual commitment to change		Commitment to the plan		Strong support		Restored trust		Necessary decisions, revised plans, progress, reappointment
New president appointed	>	Strategic plan	>	Reaction to change	>	Implementation	>	Progress review	>
		Superficial agreement		Shallow buy-in		Vacillation		Growing disaffection	Loss of trust, momentum and maybe position

Two Board-President Relationships in Times of Change
Oberlin College • Widener University

Oberlin College and Widener University provide enlightening examples of boards and presidents whose relationships have helped build stronger institutions. At Oberlin, the board worked with the president near the end of her tenure to initiate change that would restore competitiveness to the college, which had experienced three demoralizing years of budget cuts. Change at Widener focused on rebuilding the board, hiring a new president who could articulate and implement a vision to revitalize the campus, and developing a sense of civic engagement among students—all signaling the intent to restore the university's relationship with its community. In both cases, a strategic-planning process was the first step in forging a strong partnership between the board and president, which in turn enabled the leadership team to guide its institution through a notable transition. And in both instances, the board reengineered its own work and structure to facilitate its role in contributing to change.

(For more on change at Oberlin College and Widener University, see Appendix.)

AGB PRESS

Lessons about Shared Governance

Recognize occasions when the board must step forward to initiate change.

Each change process began with the board's awareness that the institution faced serious problems. At Oberlin, financial difficulties following the recession of the early 2000s, along with the erosion of the college's reputation, motivated the board's transition from a strict focus on fiduciary duties to a culture that also valued strategic thinking. At Widener, turmoil on campus, isolation from the surrounding neighborhood, and declining enrollment were the incentive for hiring a president with the imagination and experience to cure such malaise.

The surge of energy to make Oberlin more competitive with its peers and give it a sustainable business model came from the board itself, and especially from its eventual chairman Robert S. Lemle. Lemle and the board worked closely with President Nancy Dye and her successor Marvin Krislov, but there is little doubt that the impetus for change originated in the board room. At Widener, the board certainly sensed that the institution needed change, including a new relationship with the surrounding community. Blessed with a gifted chair, David W. Oskin, Widener's board became stronger before and during President's James T. Harris's tenure. But in partial contrast to Oberlin, at Widener the president took the lead by articulating and then guiding the implementation of a fresh vision for the university in response to the board's perceptions.

Understand that refreshing the vision is a joint effort.

At Oberlin, the president and an energetic board member were full partners in the process of reestablishing the university and co-chaired the strategic planning effort. At Widener, the board understood that it faced complex, interconnected issues— divisions in the academic community, the beleaguered neighborhood, competitive threats—but looked to a new president from outside to redefine the vision and reposition the university to address these problems. Widener's chair strengthened the board's membership and ensured board support for the president's change agenda.

Be prepared to work closely with the faculty.

Investing time with the faculty on the front end of the change process will pay dividends over the long term. Good ideas and strong relationships will emerge from a positive working relationship between the board and the faculty. Moreover, academic improvement comes only from capable, motivated faculty members interacting with able and willing students.

Topics for Board and President Discussion

1. ***Need for change.*** Do the board and the president agree that change is required? Have they objectively examined the hard evidence, such as trends in enrollment, revenue, graduation rates, admissions yields, and revenues to justify the need for change and its direction? Have they sought advice from outsiders with experience in similar situations?

2. ***Mutual understandings of change.*** Are the goals clear to both parties? Are the basic strategies and metrics mutually understood? If the change has been in progress for some time, have both the board and president discussed what is working well and what isn't, and have they considered adjustments based on experience?

3. ***Partnership roles.*** Have the board and the president discussed their working relationship as partners with different roles in bringing about change? For a new president, are there concerns to be aired that the board will be too intrusive or too detached? For a veteran, are there changes in the president's and the board's roles that should be discussed? Is there mutual agreement about who does what in the course of the change process? Do both the board and the president believe that candid feedback will not jeopardize their relationship?

4. ***Stakeholder engagement.*** Have the board and the president discussed how to engage other stakeholders—for example, faculty members, administrators, students, alumni, neighbors, opinion makers, legislators, and donors—in the process? If the process is well along, are the board and the president satisfied with the level of stakeholder engagement? Depending on the kind of change at hand, should one or more of these groups become more involved?

5. ***Potential obstacles and risks.*** Looking to the future, what decisions or reactions to decisions should the board and the president be prepared to manage? Since criticism and pushback are nearly inevitable, what can be done now to prepare for and ameliorate conflict? What other obstacles and risks does the change agenda face, and what strategies should the board and the president pursue to address them?

Chapter 4

BOARDS AS GAME CHANGERS

Board members can make a college or university a better place by exerting the right pressures in the right ways at the right times. Like the Roman Centurion who could order soldiers to come or go at his command, occasionally board members exercise blunt authority. But much more often, they employ a mix of toughness, sensitivity, and, like the Centurion, humility. Board members are most successful as change agents when they choose tools from their repertoire that match the demands of the situation and the pace of change. Effective change leadership also requires the board to be brutally honest in appraising its own commitment and capacity.

The board can't change the game alone. Its most important partner is the president, and other stakeholders—especially the faculty—are essential allies (see Chapter 3). There are a few changes only the board can accomplish, such as improving its own processes and evaluating and developing its membership. In other instances, the board may determine the outcome—hiring a new president, for example—but almost always, it operates with the advice and usually the implied consent of other stakeholders.

Setting strategic direction is another illustration of collaborative decision making that encourages contributions from many stakeholders while making it clear who makes the final call. Board leadership and engagement are essential, but so is working with the president, other administrative and academic leaders, faculty members, students, and community members. The board may approve major curriculum changes and the addition or elimination of academic programs, for example, but it defers to the faculty voice. It sets institutional budget priorities, but only after extensive discussion with the president and with deference to his or her recommendations about budget allocations.

This chapter focuses on the board's role in guiding the change process. It addresses the following topics:

- Choosing from a repertoire of roles in contributing to positive change;
- Matching board leadership actions with the nature of change and the institution's stage in the change process;
- Acting as consultants, managers, and vendors; and
- Assessing the board's willingness and competence to contribute to change.

Board experiences at the Thunderbird School of Global Management and Hendrix College illustrate the ideas and principles in this chapter. These very different institutions—one offering post-baccalaureate degrees in international business and the other providing a distinctive liberal arts education—show how thoughtful and energetic board members can step up to the plate to respond to a crisis, then adjust their behavior as their task moves beyond crisis management and through the stages of change.

The Board's Repertoire of Change Roles

The traditional image of board members sitting apart from the action of change, wisely dispensing judgment on proposals presented by a cordial but diffident president, is inaccurate. To be sure, prudence, good judgment, and the right amount of gravitas are traits to be treasured in a board. But many energetic boards leaven their talent for dispassionate judgment with plenty of lively and often humor-filled debate.

Board leadership in change must be both active and reflective. Ronald A. Heifetz underscores this duality with the metaphor of the balcony overlooking the dance floor. When "engaged in the dance," he points out, "it is nearly impossible to get a sense of the patterns." To perceive the larger picture, "we have to stop moving and get to the balcony."[6] Boards commit their intelligence and experience to active involvement in change, but at the same time they maintain objectivity and some distance—look on from the balcony—to ensure that energetic activity leads to real results.

Board change leaders step into different roles at different times for different purposes. Change-adept boards drive or contribute to the creation of better institutions in two complementary ways: first, by contributing the intellectual capital that stimulates or forces change, and second, by assuming the oversight authority that keeps the change process on course.

Intellectual Capital: Brain Power and Perspective

The conceptual contributions of boards derive from their experience outside and within the academy. Board members who are or have been leaders of complex organizations or academics with firsthand understanding of change in colleges and universities both can apply their knowledge and intelligence to fostering change. Board members with ties to alumni, taxpayers, political leaders, and the external community in general can offer an astute read on how a proposed change will play in the outside world. Those with the savvy to span the boundaries between the college and its environment bring important insights to discussions of change.

[6] Heifetz, *Leadership Without Easy Answers*, p. 253.

A liberal arts college typically has a thin administration in business, finance, and marketing. I relied on the talents of the board, with whom I worked well, because they were familiar. They were colleagues. When I arrived, the sense of crisis was palpable, and the board felt very strongly that its job was to make me successful. They felt vested in the success of the college.

—MARY BROWN BULLOCK, President Emerita, Agnes Scott College

Forming or Contributing to a Fresh Vision

Sometimes a visionary board member who cares deeply for the institution or the cause will imagine a new mission or way of operating that transforms a college or university. Daniel L. Ritchie, board chair and later chancellor of the University of Denver (not one of the institutions in our study), first envisioned an exceptional institution in the foothills of the Rockies and then invested millions of his own dollars and years of his life in making that aspiration a reality. In the process, he transformed a debt-ridden institution into a financially stable and academically robust university. Ritchie was unusual because he moved from the boardroom to the president's office, but his personal generosity and intense devotion to the university are typical of exceptional board leaders who contribute time, wisdom, and treasure to advancing the institutions they govern.

Focusing Attention

By influencing the meeting agenda, demanding good answers to tough questions, and returning as often as necessary to the unresolved difficulties facing the institution, board members can concentrate attention at the leadership level on the problems at hand. Sometimes one or two persistent individuals gradually force the whole board, and eventually the institution, to look at a crucial issue. Board leaders at Hendrix are properly credited with realizing early on that the "perfect storm" of reduced state scholarship aid to students, a stronger and more competitive nearby flagship state university, and the effects of September 11 on the college's endowment demanded the attention of the campus if their liberal arts college was to continue to prosper. Hendrix board leaders and the president also shared a positive entrepreneurial vision of a stronger college with a more diversified student market. Board members at Thunderbird, many of them alumni and experienced business leaders, also demanded that the sudden drop in enrollment of international students following the September 11 attacks and the SARS epidemic receive top attention from administrators and faculty.

Challenging Prevailing Wisdom

A few board members at Johnson & Wales—the national culinary, hospitality, and business university—questioned the assumption that JWU should continue to pursue growth in numbers. Throughout its modern history, the university had been run like a business, emphasizing expansion along three dimensions: enrollment, degree offerings, and geographic reach. This former secretarial school once had as many as eight separate national and international campuses and offered everything from certificates to doctoral degrees. In a bold departure from this strategy, board members challenged the president to pursue improvements in quality over expansion and growth. As a result, the university raised the bar for incoming students, adopted a more strategic approach to program development, reduced the number of campuses, and began looking at metrics like retention and graduation rates to gauge success.

Importing Fresh Perspectives

Board members who have led major enterprises often are the best people to contribute fresh ideas on the business side of a college or university. When it comes to rebuilding a broken or fractured business model, engineering an operational turnaround, or making strategic financial decisions, current or former senior executives with experience in strategy making, finance, marketing, or information systems have much to offer. The Thunderbird board realized that conventional institution-wide cuts would not make up for a 50 percent drop in enrollment at this tuition-dependent school. The board led the way in major initiatives—reducing the faculty from 120 to 40 and developing market-oriented new programs in executive business education—that eventually put Thunderbird on a more stable fiscal base.

Partnering in Testing and Creating New Ideas

"I need time to 'think out loud' with the board," explained one public university president in describing how he used small private meetings with board members to explore innovations and test ideas. To promote the exploration of sensitive topics without the chilling effect of publicity from an open meeting, he reached an agreement with journalists that they would not attend, with the understanding that they would be informed quickly as discussion moved closer to decision making.

The questions at these sessions were important ones to the future of the university: If we were designing the university today, how would it be different? Should we develop an online unit without the usual departments and full-time staff? College X continues to lose enrollment, and its graduates have difficulty finding jobs. Is it time to phase it out? Thinking out loud around questions like these allowed the president to get the board's best views and analysis of politically and operationally complex issues.

The University of Dubuque formalizes such give-and-take in two-day annual educational seminars at which the president and the board vigorously debate alternative futures for the institution. In addition to engendering a strong sense of participation in the university's strategic directions, these meetings give both the board and the president a clearer sense of their respective views and help them reach consensus on critical decisions about admissions thresholds, branding strategies, academic programs to emphasize, and other key issues.

Oversight Authority: The Buck Stops with the Board

Contributing first-rate, fresh ideas to discussions of strategy and tactics is one vital part of the board's role in change. Even more significant is the power inherent in the board's governing authority. Boards may lack the aura attributed by Lloyd's of London to the ship's master—"captain under God"—but they do have potent moral and legal authority. When the board devotes visible attention to a challenge—such as the enrollment and financial decline at Thunderbird or the prospect of the same at Hendrix—the institution takes notice. By the same token, a board that blithely ignores signs of trouble engenders a similar passivity. Change-adept boards can exercise their informal and formal authority in a number of ways, as illustrated below.

Monitoring Progress

Academics are famous for devising grandiose plans and then proceeding to skip the essential steps that convert ideas into reality. Boards and presidents working together can insist on metrics and progress reports to show whether or not change is actually taking place. Most of the institutions that AGB studied had developed such metrics. One option is a dashboard report that monitors key performance indicators in a consistent format and highlights warning signs, such as a sudden drop in applications or acceptances of students. Other measures include longer-term trend lines that track past performance and forecast probable future trends.

At Hendrix College, after trending forecasts revealed that a newly competitive state university could have a negative impact on Hendrix's ability to continue attracting top students, the board coupled analysis with action. It worked with the new president and faculty to develop Hendrix's signature Odyssey program, which encourages students to engage in educational pursuits tailored to their interests and talents in areas like global awareness and artistic creativity. Several empirical studies have shown that this distinctive learning experience enabled the college to maintain its appeal to superior applicants, grow enrollment by 50 percent, and capture a greater share of its market.

Galvanizing Others to Action

When there is no president in place, or the president is unable to lead in the face of urgency, it is up to the board to galvanize action. Failure to step into the leadership vacuum in dire circumstances is a breakdown in the board's duty to preserve the institution. Even with presidential leadership, the board can play a catalytic role in prompting action. Thunderbird's engaged board brought key players together to handle an emergency that threatened institutional survival, an example of a board's intellectual and authoritative roles reinforcing one another. The decision to make drastic reductions in world-language faculty, coupled with the new requirement that incoming students display foreign-language competence, was a fresh way of reinforcing Thunderbird's international character without the costs associated with language instruction. To make that idea work, however, the board needed the decision-making authority to eliminate 80 faculty positions. Good ideas coupled with the power to make them happen represent the combined effects of the cognitive and authoritative strengths of an effective board.

Making the Tough Calls

Hard and courageous decisions by a responsible board can jump-start change, help sustain momentum, or even, as with Goddard College in Vermont, force solutions to dire problems. Goddard, the one-time icon of progressive education, had fallen on hard times as competition for students increased and career preparation replaced revolutionary ideas in the minds of undergraduates. The college's survival as an independent institution was in doubt. The board—led by the chair, who was a graduate of the historic undergraduate program—chose to eliminate the residential option in favor of a low-residency alternative for adults. The college began to grow and its budget moved safely into the black, but this relative prosperity would not have come about without hard decisions by responsible board members.

Knowing When to Say No

"No" is not a bad word when it comes to turning down an ill-considered proposal. Depending on the author of the proposal, it may be that only the board can say it. At the University of Dubuque, for example, the board and the president discussed the option of affiliating with a proprietary college to secure much-needed additional revenue. After considerable debate, the board chose to remain true to the mission—to "be what we were created to be," in the words of the chair—rather than to engage in a joint venture with a partnership that many felt was inconsistent with Dubuque's faith-based culture. The institution went on to accomplish a splendid turnaround by emphasizing what made it worth preserving in the first place. For example, its externally funded Wendt Character Initiative enables faculty members to inculcate a culture of character study and development throughout their students' educational experience.

Healing the Wounded

Bringing major change to famously change-adverse organizations can be a dangerous business for college presidents. Pushback is a euphemism for what can be vicious personal attacks, public demonstrations, and highly publicized votes of no confidence. Boards can and should take some of the heat that the stress of change engenders. Individual members can also provide personal support to a beleaguered president and other members of the change team who have put their careers and their standing in the academic community on the line for the sake of positive, if painful, change.

Confirming the New Order

At the end of the change process and at points in between, it is the board that must vote on and endorse the adjustments in programs, policies, and organizational structure that emerge. Short of the courts and the legislature (in the case of public colleges and universities), the board is the final governing authority. Their formal approval, recorded in the minutes and often reported in the news media, makes permanent the new order of things. Most of the functions listed above are collaborative efforts. This final act is the board's responsibility alone.

How to Deal with Misguided Board Behavior

So far this chapter has touted the benefits of fresh ideas and perspectives contributed by intelligent boards that also are willing to exercise their governing authority in appropriate ways to guide change. But what can be done when board members try using their authority to push ill-considered or untimely ideas? Three remedies will help short-circuit such efforts.

First, a strong chair can remind the obstreperous crew that only the whole board decides for the board. The chair can also issue regular reminders that ideas proposed by board members must run the same intellectual gauntlet and be subject to the same rigorous scrutiny as ideas from any other source. Finally, teams of board members, administrators, and sometimes faculty members can temper the impulse of any one person to dominate. Metro State, for example, developed the public-private partnership that led to its Hotel and Hospitality Learning Center by employing a team of trustees with expertise in urban development, law, and the politics of these complex initiatives.

Choosing Board Leadership Roles to Suit the Change Cycle

Change leadership requires the creativity to imagine a new way of doing business that is better adapted to altered circumstances. It also requires discipline in knowing when to initiate, lead, monitor, question, and confirm—and when to get out of the way. As the repertoire of change roles suggests, boards can lead and participate constructively in many ways. There is a fine art to selecting the role that suits the change process as a whole and is appropriate for the institution's specific stage in that process. Change-adept boards do not become less engaged as the impetus for change passes and stability returns. Instead, their focus shifts from galvanizing themselves and the institution into action to a more reflective posture requiring such intellectual and social skills as sound judgment, effective interpersonal communication, and solid relationships.

John P. Kotter's eight-step change process provides a framework for aligning change tools with the unfolding change process (Figure 4.1). We break this model into three phases: beginning, middle, and ending. During the beginning phase, boards and other change leaders concentrate on bringing attention to the crisis, assembling and motivating a team to address it, and developing initial strategies. This work is cerebral and interactive. Reflecting, evaluating alternative solutions, discarding some, selecting others, and building the change team all must come before plunging into the action of change. Sustaining the change process is the work of the middle phase. The board stays involved in change, but its role as monitor and sustainer of the work replaces the brainstorming elements of the beginning phase. The ending of one period of change almost always sets the stage for the start of a new round. But a declaration of victory through some formal board action—endorsing the Odyssey program at Hendrix for example—is an important public event that signals real change has occurred in the life of the institution.

Figure 4.1 Kotter's Eight Phases of Change

PHASES OF CHANGE	POSSIBLE BOARD ACTIONS
BEGINNING	
1. Establish a sense of urgency.	Bring attention to the crisis.
2. Assemble guiding coalitions.	Galvanize a change team.
3. Develop a new vision and select strategies.	Become better informed. Contribute to a vision. Challenge conventional solutions. Critique proposed strategies. Seek metrics of success. Support emerging strategies.
MIDDLE	
4. Communicate the change vision.	Use the board pulpit to support it.
5. Empower broad-based action.	Showcase change leaders.
6. Generate short-term wins.	Recognize achievements. Act as thought leaders and partners.
7. Consolidate gains.	Confirm interim changes. Monitor progress.
END (AND BEGINNING CHANGE AGAIN)	
8. Anchor new approaches.	Confirm new approaches in policy. Take formal action. Review achievements. Renew the change process.

Adapted from John P. Kotter, *Leading Change* (Harvard Business School Press, 1996).

Ways to Tap into Board Expertise

Board engagement in high-level strategic discussions that lead to change is an accepted role. But how active should board members become on the operational side, and under what conditions? In the three examples that follow, the board was instrumental in operations that supported strategic objectives—freeing up resources to build institutional reputation, developing real estate to make the campus environment more attractive, and running a campaign to rebrand a college.

At first blush, having a sitting board member provide consulting services to the institution, manage the operations of a major or minor initiative, or sell a service or product to the institution would all seem ill advised. At public institutions in most states, payment for such services would be prima facie evidence of a conflict of interest. State law and regulation would declare them illegal. Even when those relationships were allowed, governance purists would argue that consulting runs the risk of crossing the line between policy and management. Is it even possible, much less advisable, to set aside the board member's authority to become an employee or contractor even if the service is free, expert, and much needed?

The following three experiences confirm that board members can act as unpaid consultants without damaging their board roles when the process is fully transparent, temporary, and approved formally by the board.

Consulting Board Members

The College of New Jersey (TCNJ) board takes its responsibility for financial stewardship seriously. In 1998, as the action rate bond market was going through a significant period of deterioration, the board, in partnership with the president and treasurer, led an effort to restructure the institution's debt portfolio to fixed rate. Throughout this complicated and time-sensitive process, the board was consulted regularly and provided the guidance to ensure that the transaction went smoothly. The financial acumen of a handful of board members was essential to making certain that all board members understood the risks and benefits to the current structure, as well as the advantages of refinancing. The support and reassurance provided by those board members demonstrated how governing boards and administration can leverage the expertise of individual trustees in a cooperative way. In 2008, because the portfolio had been converted to fixed rate, TCNJ avoided the extremely negative impact experienced by many academic institutions.

Managing Partners

Several Hendrix College board members, with the endorsement of the entire board, have been working closely with the president on developing some significant acreage adjacent to the campus. The board considered selling the property, but it has decided instead to develop the plan for the Village at Hendrix, which combines academic buildings with residential and retail development. The entire project may net more than $80 million, while adding appealing amenities for residents and students that Conway, Ark., currently does not offer. As noted earlier, a team including a savvy board member experienced in real-estate development, the president, and others oversees this project on behalf of the board as a whole.

Vendors

Lionel Sosa, a board member who was the founder of the nation's largest Hispanic advertising agency, engaged his firm to lead the repositioning of the University of the Incarnate Word in San Antonio, Tex. (not one of the institutions we studied). This comprehensive marketing effort included focus groups at Incarnate Word, creative services, and advertising placement. The agency's billings would likely have been beyond the reach of a struggling independent college, but it agreed to accept a dollar-for-dollar trade of services for scholarships. Since the college had excess capacity in its classes, it incurred no new costs as a result of this arrangement. Louis Agnese, the college president, points to a near tripling of overall enrollment in 12 years and a 155-percent increase in Hispanic enrollment as evidence of the campaign's success.

As these examples demonstrate, boards can venture into the management realm when certain conditions apply:

- Board members have genuine expertise that would be expensive or hard to find elsewhere.
- Outside consulting services would be prohibitively expensive for the institution.
- The work is central to the mission and clearly driven by institutional need.
- The board as a whole discusses, understands, and approves this exception to separating management from policy making.
- The incursion into operations is project oriented or task oriented, and it is temporary.

Assessing Board Capacity

When it comes to leading or contributing to positive change, there is a sweet spot that rests between reluctance to lead and excessive enthusiasm. Before a board commits itself to a major role in the change process, members should discuss where the sweet spot is for them and their institution.

Boards can be averse, prone, and adept when it comes to change (Figure 4.2). The change-averse group is hesitant to endorse change or engage in it themselves. Perhaps captive to external interests—athletic boosters, alumni infatuated with the college they experienced years before, academics wedded to a traditional educational model—the change-averse board allows itself to worry more about the reaction to change than the consequences of avoiding it. It may be in denial over the real challenges, insisting that long-term downward trends are really cyclical and that a turnaround will come without their intervention. At the other extreme is the board that is overly prone to change, itching to pull the trigger on new projects without the patience to see the results of yesterday's initiative. When change does not occur as fast as it would like, this kind of board quickly looks for a scapegoat—usually the president.

Finding the middle way between timidity and brashness, the change-adept board looks for hard evidence that change is in order. It devotes time to understanding the institution and its situation—the beginning phase described in Figure 4.1—before embarking on a change journey. It regularly considers its appropriate role in change and its working relationships, especially with its partner in change, the president.

Transitioning a change-prone board into an adept one often means reining in overactive members without dampening their enthusiasm. Moving from a change-averse board to one more able to guide change requires leaders who patiently explain the need for change to current members and seek new members who realize that guiding change is often a necessary board responsibility.

Thunderbird's board appears to have been change-adept from the start. When the enrollment crisis hit, members versed in the competitive, quick-response world of business were poised to cut costs and mount new programs. At Hendrix a farsighted chair began rebuilding the board several years before the crises described here, involving experienced leaders prepared to understand a real threat to the college and to take prompt action.

Figure 4.2 How Boards Contribute to Change

	LEAST ENGAGED		OVERACTIVE
	Change Reluctant (or Averse)	Change Adept	Change Prone
Relationship with President	Relies on president to initiate and lead change Reluctant to conduct in-depth presidential assessment	Challenges and supports the president	Creates a "coping" response from the president
Role of Chair	Chair focused exclusively on board harmony	Chair sees change leadership as major responsibility	Chair fails to rein in overly creative members Board fails to rein in overly creative chair
Board Dynamics	Small number of board members control board and institution Seeks to avoid blame and criticism	Regularly discusses board-president's role in change process Adjusts behavior in tune with stages of change	Pursues hobby horses Intolerant of criticism of their proposals
Other Stakeholders	Supports constituent interests over institutional needs	Engages faculty and others in change process	Discounts input from others
Understanding of Strategy	Tied to current business model	Insists on measures of performance and forecasts Alert to need for change in competitive environment	Cannot distinguish between strategy and operations
Approach to Change	Prefers "peace in the valley" to stress of change Satisfied with incremental improvement	Experienced in change management in complex organizations Recognizes that greatest risk may lie in no change Sees change as key to long-term institutional vitality Actively contributes ideas and proposals for change	Prefers change for its own sake Generates too many ideas too often Lacks a filter to evaluate new ideas More intrigued with a new idea than evaluating the success of current ones

Two Change-Adept Boards
Thunderbird School of Global Management • Hendrix College

The narratives of change at Thunderbird School of Global Management and Hendrix College illuminate the use of a crisis as a springboard to building a stronger institution. At Thunderbird, the crisis was immediate and threatening to the institution's very existence. The board drove the actions that rescued it: reducing costs and diversifying the program mix while retaining Thunderbird's position as a top provider of international business education. Board members remain highly engaged in strategy and operations. Hendrix's board, which can be described as change-adept but not change-prone, anticipated a crisis based on shifts in the competitive environment. Board members were prepared to lead change when the situation demanded it. Working in partnership with a new president, the board contributes mightily to the continuing renewal of the college.

Both institutions have emerged from periods of serious threat in strong or stronger positions. Thunderbird might have gone under were it not for timely board intervention at the start of the downward slide. Today, it remains at the top in business-school rankings. Hendrix's achievements in becoming a more attractive institution with greater private support speak volumes for the salutary effects of greater board involvement.

What might have happened without board engagement is a matter of speculation. Did board members fill a leadership vacuum that some unknown hero might have occupied? It is hard to imagine who that masked man might have been or where he might have come from. Our conclusion is that both Thunderbird and Hendrix were fortunate to have strong board leaders in place when events turned against them.

(For more on change at Thunderbird School of Global Management and Hendrix College, see Appendix.)

Lessons about the Board's Role in Change

Several factors contributed to success for the boards of these two institutions. Their stories reflect qualities that other change-oriented boards might consider and emulate.

Bring the right people with the right expertise on board.

Both boards were remarkably well equipped to address the competitive and environmental threats. The Thunderbird board, as one observer put it, amounted to a virtual "Who's Who" in international business. Members brought real expertise, not just opinion, to the table. The rapid enrollment decline took the board by surprise, but they responded with practical, tough-minded solutions, such as dismissing 80 faculty members once the scope of the catastrophe became clear.

Hendrix's board membership had been invigorated by the addition of business and nonprofit leaders several years before the crisis. This high-functioning group was ready when all their talents were called for. The lesson, developed further in Chapter 6, is to make board recruitment and training a high priority so that talent is available and members are prepared when a crisis hits.

Generate exceptional personal commitment from board members.

These boards displayed a high degree of dedication to their respective institutions. Although both included a high percentage of alumni, enthusiasm was contagious among all members—prompting those new to the board to quickly embrace the college as one of their top priorities. Building enthusiasm among new board members and sustaining it among veterans doesn't happen without thoughtful effort, usually on the part of the chair and the president.

At Hendrix and Thunderbird, involving board members in meaningful work was the chief vehicle for building and nurturing engagement. In assigning members to committees, for example, the board chairs took pains to respond to members' interests. Experienced mentors helped newcomers learn how the board functioned. Perhaps most important, both chairs ensured that board and committee meetings were forums for discussion and debate about the future of the institution. Board members said that they looked forward to attending meetings. One Hendrix board member observed that she had resigned from a different board where listening to long reports and then voting approval were the norm. Instead, she chose the Hendrix experience, which stimulated her best thinking in spirited dialogue with smart colleagues over the future of an important institution.

Make teamwork part of board culture.

Both boards functioned as teams to comprehend the depth of the challenges and discuss alternative resolutions. Both enjoyed the benefits of strong, engaged chairs and individual board members whose professional commitments allowed them to devote extra time to board service. Both reported an "all hands on deck" attitude toward redeeming and strengthening their institutions.

Change-focused governance is a team sport. Contributing to this sense of teamwork are group discussions, ad hoc task forces with several members who later engage the whole board in conversation around their task, and committee work linked with board policy. Tying task-group work to full board discussions sustains collective engagement in the pros and cons of a major project.

Building cohesion and a collaborative work ethic among board members from the start ensures that a team is in place to handle emergencies. At Thunderbird, board members functioned together like the competent business leaders they were in their professional lives to assess the situation calmly and quickly and then take timely action. The Hendrix board agreed from the start that the external threats demanded strategic response. Board members galvanized the college community—not just the board, but faculty and staff member—around purposeful action.

Make board service feel compelling.

At Hendrix, the Methodist heritage remains vital. Bylaws require that the board include several clergy. Board members had rejected what they saw as overly doctrinaire faith requirements earlier in the college's history because they were committed to the mainstream Protestant values that Hendrix embodied. Enabling board members to realize that their work is part of a higher calling, and that our higher-education system is one of the glories of our society, helps build the level of commitment needed to sustain change. If Hendrix board members saw their work as part of a larger social and religious commitment, they also believed the college's vision and values were compelling.

Thunderbird is not a faith-based institution, but many board members felt that the value of their board membership transcended governing a first-rate business school. They understood the importance of business in international relations, and they genuinely embraced the view that "borders frequented by trade seldom need soldiers." They appreciated the school's role, as one put it, as "a force for positive economic and social change."

Build appreciation for the equilibrium of governance.

To varying degrees, both boards are attentive to the governance equilibrium among the board, the president, and the institution. Thunderbird board members realize that they are more engaged in the workings of the school than most boards would find comfortable or appropriate—indeed, many students of governance would find this board to be too active in operations. But the balance between executive and board authority seems to work. The president says that he values the opportunity to partner with his engaged board and that he and the chair talk frankly about the line between policy and management.

Governance at Hendrix represents a balanced and mature relationship between the president and his board. Meetings feature lively debate among board members and between board members and the president over important governance issues: Does growth involve the risk of losing the college's identity? Does work on the Village at Hendrix distract the president and the board from the institution's fundamental educational mission? Are some board members too engaged in the operational side of this real-estate development and other aspects of college operations?

Match board action to the stages of change.

To some extent, the Hendrix and Thunderbird boards adjusted their behavior as the change process took hold. Both stepped into a leadership vacuum at the beginning of their respective crises and then gradually shifted to behaviors that balanced engagement with observation and reflection—roles appropriate to the middle phase of change (see Figure 4.1). Unlike change-prone board members who cannot resist taking executive action, these boards respect the domain of the president without being afraid to debate, challenge, and guide their executives.

Topics for Board and President Discussion

1. *Intellectual capital.* How well do we as a board apply our intellectual capital and perspectives along with our governance authority in fostering positive change?

2. *Leading the board.* How effective are we as a board-president team in orchestrating the board's contribution of ideas to guide change and its assertion of authority to bring about change?

3. *Board change behavior.* How has the board adjusted its leadership behavior to reflect the beginning, middle, and ending stages of the change process?

4. *Lending board talents.* How effective is the board at enabling members with special talents to assist the change process without becoming inappropriately involved in operations?

5. *Change leadership style.* To what degree is this board averse to, adept at, or overly prone to change?

Chapter 5

WORKING WITH BOARDS ON CHANGE: ADVICE TO PRESIDENTS

Most college and university presidents are hired today with the expectation that they will lead change. Candidates should be wary of the board that says that the status quo is just fine and the president's job is to preserve it. They are likely hearing what board members and other stakeholders prefer to be true, not what the real challenges are. Far more likely, however, the board knows that the institution requires changes, although the nature and direction of that change may not be clear. It looks to the new leader to work with board members and the campus community to solve old problems and forge new directions. Most veteran presidents, too, face the need to lead change that was scarcely envisioned when they began their jobs.

An effective relationship with the board, while always central to leadership, is crucial if a president is to fulfill the expectation to bring about a new order. Cultivating the relationship goes well beyond the logistics of communication and collaboration. It begins with building both self-awareness and awareness of the institution's needs. Presidents should have a clear understanding of the kind of change situation they face, the board's preparedness to participate, and their own capacity to work with board members, faculty members, and other stakeholders on and off campus. New and experienced presidents alike should join with their boards to map plans and schedules and to consider how they will handle the inevitable pushback to new initiatives. Achieving these understandings will vastly increase the odds of successful change and a more satisfying presidential tenure.

This chapter guides presidents in developing a relationship with the board that supports and strengthens a change process. It builds on earlier discussions about the dynamics of change (Chapter 1), the essential relationship between the president and the board (Chapter 3), and the repertoire of board roles in change (Chapter 4). It is organized around four questions that every president, new on the job or veteran, should consider:

- What kinds of changes will the institution require in light of the challenges it faces today and in the foreseeable future?
- How can the board become better prepared to play a major role in the change process?
- Is the president open to learning about his strengths and weaknesses when it comes to bringing change to the institution?
- What issues surrounding change do the president and board need to discuss before launching a change agenda?

The chapter begins with a cautionary tale about a hypothetical institution where a well-intentioned change process went off track because of presidential missteps. In contrast, two board-president relationships that advance change are discussed at the end of the chapter. Since Roosevelt University's board hired Charles R. Middleton as president in 2002, this Chicago institution has emerged as an urban university that is committed to high quality while sustaining its dedication to educational access. The board of Metropolitan State College of Denver invited Stephen M. Jordan to become president in 2005 with the mandate to increase the college's educational performance and enhance its stature in the community.

A Cautionary Tale

There are many examples of presidents who came to grief because they failed to consider all the angles seriously before they plunged into a change process. Consider this cautionary tale, which is a composite of several presidential misfires.

> *A bright young president begins his tenure vowing to move his comprehensive university to the next level of excellence. He believes strongly that the board supports his vision even if board members do not completely understand it. Indeed, when the board interviewed and hired him, it admired his vigorous, energetic persona—a marked contrast to that of his staid predecessor. For several years before his arrival, a vague sense of malaise pervaded the campus and the boardroom. Indicators suggested that the institution was losing ground to its competitors. When his predecessor left of his own accord, the board sought a more energetic new leader, but had only general thoughts about new directions that leader might pursue.*

> *At first, board members cheered the new president's plan to move the campus up in the rankings, make it more competitive with its historic peers, raise more money for the endowment, and boost research activity. Some board members, and many faculty members, told him that the athletics budget was out of control. The new president let it be known that he intended to correct that problem, too.*

> *But soon some faculty members and alumni were grumbling that the new president had moved too far, too fast. Faculty members felt they had not been sufficiently consulted about new directions, and alumni, including a few board members, began to question the president's appreciation of the importance of athletics to student recruitment and fund raising. The faculty senate's executive committee requested a private meeting with the board, without the president, to discuss their concerns. The president's glowing reports to the board masked increasing discontent with change. One board member suggested that the board move up the date of the president's evaluation to "send him a message" that the board felt change was being foisted on the campus too quickly.*

What went wrong? The intent of this chapter is to answer that question and to help other presidents avoid this too-common predicament. It seems clear that this new president failed to assess the campus's or the board's readiness to engage in change, and perhaps his own change leadership capacity as well. This case holds lessons not only for neophytes, but also for veteran presidents. The veteran enjoys the advantage of knowing the institution and having established positive relationships with the board and the campus community, but he or she faces special challenges when it comes to leading change that was not anticipated at the start. Few presidents expected the sharp drops in endowments and public support occasioned by the recent recession, much less the brand of leadership that this "new normal" required. A president who began the job with the expectation of boosting fund raising, for example, will need to adjust both strategies and personal style if the mandate becomes reducing costs. The veteran may also need to overcome the board's perceptions of her strengths and weaknesses to persuade them that she can lead when the agenda for change itself changes. This recasting is vital to the president's success if she is, justifiably or not, blamed for a decline or crisis that now must be remedied.

Presidents who serve long terms successfully are able to reinvent themselves periodically as leadership needs change. James C. Votruba, president since 1997 of the fast-growing Northern Kentucky University, keeps his presidency fresh by discussing seminal questions with his board: If we were building this university from scratch, knowing what we face today, how would we do it differently?

Another aid to redirecting the veteran presidency is to enlarge the periodic 360-degree evaluation that most boards require of presidents in their fourth or fifth year of service. This evaluation should include a review of past performance, of course, but to help the president and the board adjust to the latest challenges, it should give equal attention to what kind of change leadership both should assert going forward. Taking full advantage of this future-oriented assessment demands a president who is open to advice, even criticism, and emotionally and intellectually agile in adjusting to new circumstances.

> *"Change means movement, movement means friction, friction means heat, and heat means controversy. The only place where there is no friction is in outer space or a seminar on political action."*
> —SAUL ALINSKY, *Rules for Radicals* (Random House, 1971)

Diagnosing the Kind of Change Required

An incoming president needs to penetrate a barrage of information to learn a few important realities quickly. Does the change demand a serious rethinking of institutional traditions, values, and mission, or is it less dramatic and unlikely to require profound adaptation? How has the institution addressed change in the past, and how prepared is it to take on new challenges? How can the president help the campus community engage positively in the change process? If change is already underway, where does the process stand, how is it progressing, and what level of support does it enjoy? Perhaps most important, the new president needs to learn whether his predecessor's departure was connected to change.

Sitting presidents should address many of the same questions. They should be especially alert to the opportunities for fresh leadership occasioned by the entry of new board members or experienced board members elected to leadership posts. Whether or not the institution requires a periodic 360-degree evaluation for the president, it is in the president's best interest to work with the board in inviting a savvy outsider to perform an institutional and environmental scan that will provide an objective take on the institution's competitive position and strategic options. On its path to becoming one of the nation's top small Christian universities, the University of Dubuque regularly seeks outside help to decide what next level of excellence the president and board should pursue. Metro State regularly seeks outside consultants to work with its board, president, and senior staff to assess the college's performance against its strategic goals and the alignment of board work with those goals. The board rotates consultants to ensure that it receives different perspectives on its performance.

Operational or Adaptive Change?

Looking at change on the spectrum described in Chapter 2—from operational or technical change to serious adaptations in habitual ways of operating, institutional values, and perhaps even mission—Type I or operational change usually is far less threatening to the tenure of a new leader than adaptive or Type III change. (Of course, major cost overruns in implementing a relatively simple operational change, a too-common experience, can be embarrassing, or worse.) Although the president should keep the board informed about major operational innovations, active participation usually is not necessary or appropriate unless a board member has special technical knowledge that would be useful.

Change that threatens to dislodge the social equilibrium and requires sometimes-painful adaptation to uncomfortable new realities demands close board involvement rather than simple awareness. In these situations—the elimination of a cherished but no longer viable academic program, for example, or a major refocusing of the mission—"thinking out loud" with the board far upstream of the action will yield better ideas and help ensure board support during the change process.

Boards and presidents both need to be prepared for the nearly inevitable opposition that accompanies these emotionally wrought changes. When President Stephen M. Jordan proposed adding master's degrees to Metro State's baccalaureate-only repertoire of programs, this departure from tradition occasioned a robust board conversation around the impact of graduate programs on the institution's mission and purpose. Ultimately the board endorsed Jordan's plan, but only after he convinced members that it made both educational and business sense.

The Stages of Change

Leadership and change expert John P. Kotter's framework for change suggests board actions appropriate to three stages: beginning, middle, and end (see Figure 4.1). A president embarking on a change agenda will want to know more precisely where in each stage the institution lies. The boards of Roosevelt and Metro State charged their new presidents with launching change by increasing the institutions' visibility and eminence while remaining true to socially progressive missions that prized access for the underserved. Neither Roosevelt nor Metro State had been static, but both boards clearly expected the change trajectory to rise quickly when the new presidents arrived.

A new president often enters the scene, however, when change is already in progress. When Mary Brown Bullock became president of Agnes Scott College, the change instigated and led by a highly engaged board had been under way for nearly two years. Bullock was expected to contribute fresh energy and vision but not to make fundamental modifications to the strategic vision of restoring Agnes Scott to its position as an exceptional women's college. Like Bullock, Marvin Krislov at Oberlin and R. Barbara Gitenstein at The College of New Jersey joined institutions where a strategic trajectory had been established. A president entering the change drama at its midpoint will benefit from spending time with board members to learn their perspective on a process that they may have initiated.

Reenergizing an ongoing change process is different but no less demanding than beginning change. Fulfilling the potential of change begun in the face of new challenges—such as the decline in state funding that was the impetus at The College of New Jersey—or rekindling enthusiasm for continuing change in the face of change fatigue call for just as much presidential talent and creativity as launching change.

Institutional Readiness

A new leader who has run a long interview gauntlet involving representative members of the academic community and most of the board assumes the presidency with a reasonably accurate sense of the current status of change and the prevailing attitudes toward it. More-limited search processes—such as those conducted almost exclusively by a search firm and a few board members—may reveal a lot about what the board seeks in the way of change but little about campus attitudes. In both situations, more attention to diagnosing the institution's readiness for change is in order, especially when the president is just beginning to learn campus culture and opinion.

An essential first step for any new president with change in mind is determining how well the institution understands its financial strength, its competitiveness in the current market for students and financial support, and its reputation or brand among those who influence its future (not how the institution believes others view it). The board members at Metro State held high expectations for Steve Jordan's leadership. After all, they were the college's first trustees following its exit from a four-campus system with a system board, and they had devoted two years to searching for just the right leader. A native of Colorado, Jordan had a good feel for campus culture and knew some of the faculty members, but after his appointment he took great pains to meet with every unit on campus to gauge attitudes toward the new board and the potential new directions for the college. Metro State's successful transition to a college that is highly engaged with the state's higher-education CEOs and authorities, including the legislature, is testimony to Jordan's perspicacity in learning the college's readiness for change before engaging in it.

Why the Previous President Left

An instructive exercise involves understanding what led to the departure that created a splendid opportunity for a new president. If the former leader retired after years of valued service or moved on to a more attractive position, so much the better. But the truth may be at odds with the public narrative. Did the board encourage the departure because the president was unable to lead change or because he stumbled in bringing about the change the board sought? Or was he a victim of change itself and the friction occasioned by a new order? What does the departure, especially if not entirely voluntary, say about the board's expectations and patience, its understanding of the realities of change, and its sensitivity to the barricades that the academy throws up to forestall change?

The departure of American University's president in the wake of a scandal over compensation is a blatant reminder of the value of involving all board members in sensitive decisions, such as how much to pay the president. The well-publicized decision of the new board at Metro State to part company with its president after 10 years clearly indicates that the board had a different style of leadership in mind.

Returning to the hypothetical case at the beginning of this chapter, the new president made several mistakes at the start. He appears to have created a vision of what the college needed without first trying to learn what the campus community thought and felt about the need and direction of change. He also apparently failed to nurture campus or board support for the changes he pursued.

Appraising the Board's Readiness to Lead and Support Change

Just because an institution needs change does not guarantee that the board fully acknowledges the need, has the leadership to support it, or can contribute to change in a meaningful way. Early warning signs such as declining acceptance rates of qualified students, decreasing net assets, and emerging competition might indicate that change is due—or overdue. But that does not mean automatically that the board itself is ready for change. A study of turnarounds at beleaguered colleges and universities in 2006–2007 described several cases in which the board denied or ignored the need for change until faculty members or a new president called their attention to plunging indicators of institutional health.[7]

No president wants to believe that he is leading a parade of change, only to discover belatedly that he is alone in the vanguard, like the president in our hypothetical case. Careful investigation of the board's ability to play its role in leading and supporting change prevents that lonely experience.

---

[7] Terrence MacTaggart, ed., *Academic Turnarounds: Restoring Vitality to Challenged American Colleges and Universities* (American Council on Education and Greenwood, 2007).

Developing Mutual Expectations for Change Leadership

The interview is an opportunity for two-way communication in which the candidate sizes up the board while the board appraises the candidate. Scott S. Cowen confesses that before he became president of Tulane University he had turned down an offer from another institution because he felt that the board was ill equipped to support his vigorous leadership. Cowen, an expert on boards and governance, is adept at assessing a board's potential for change leadership. This background helps explain why he and two able board members set about strengthening Tulane's board soon after he joined the university in 1998, well before Katrina's floodwaters engulfed the campus in 2005.

If the periodic comprehensive evaluation of the president—preferably of the president and the board—includes a strong orientation toward the changes required to sustain institutional vitality, it offers a learning opportunity parallel to that available to new presidents during the interview. By asking an outside expert to provide an objective, or at least external, appraisal of the institution's competitive position, the board and president have another opportunity to rethink what their next steps should be. For example, accreditation reports, if the visiting team is sophisticated in understanding institutional strategy and climate, can be a springboard for president and board conversations about what ought to be the next change priorities.

Signs of Board Preparedness

Boards that show readiness to engage in change display some of these indicators:

- Board members who are executives experienced in leading complex organizations through difficult times. They tend to understand the need for organizational change and the challenges associated with it.

- A few academics on the board, including at least one former or current president, with experience in bringing change to colleges and universities. These members can help their business colleagues on the board understand that change in the academy usually takes longer and requires more participation than it does in the business world.

- A realistic strategic plan, with a few telling metrics and evidence of substantial board involvement in creating the plan and monitoring progress. Such a plan suggests that board members see the link between good ideas and methodical efforts to carry them out.

- Board members who have supported change in the recent past. Positive experience with change is a sign of how they will behave in the future, especially if the same members remain leaders on the board.

A candid conversation between the president and board members will help them assess their understanding of the complex fabric of change and their commitment to pursuing it. Do their comments show a depth of understanding of the institution and its needs? Do they seem to have good evidence of its performance? Do they appreciate the barriers to change that are unique to the academy? Do they appear willing to learn more about the institution, change in general, and their role in working with a president to make it succeed? Board members who base their views on ideology or uninformed opinion make uncomfortable change partners. Helping board members fill the gaps in their knowledge and understanding must occur before the change process begins.

Developing the Board's Capacity to Participate in Change

Experienced board leaders who know what it takes to lead change in complex organizations can help a board develop into a higher-performing group. The chair and a few board members who have several more years to serve can represent the nucleus of a change-adept board. Working as a team with the president, the board should use an intentional recruitment program to assess what kinds of skills the board needs to support change. Members with experience leading change in business, nonprofit organizations, and higher education usually are eager to engage intellectually with the president on behalf of the institution.

Sound board processes—how board members communicate, test ideas, relate to the president, and make decisions—are essential to effective change leadership. Converting board meetings from desultory exercises in patience to robust discussions of strategies and policy options is the best way to keep new, activist members engaged. The University of Dubuque, the locus of an impressive turnaround in enrollment, private giving, and campus renovation, keeps its 36-member board engaged through informed and lively policy debates at annual educational retreats and regular board meetings. Yeasty discussion about what it means in practical terms to become "the best small Christian university"—Dubuque's aspiration—punctuates these meetings. The board explores how demographic changes affect enrollment, matching the curriculum to the students' actual needs, institutional branding, and other strategically important topics. The president joins board members who are charged with board development to set the agenda.

What Jeffrey A. Sonnenfeld, a dean and professor at Yale School of Management and best-selling author of many leadership books, describes as a "virtuous cycle of respect, trust, and candor" characterizes board culture at Dubuque, Metro State, and other institutions in this study where board members are actively engaged with presidents in bringing about change. In such a culture, the president and the board challenge one another in frank debate over critical issues facing their institutions.

Working with Boards Across the Spectrum

It is impossible for a president to lead change if the board is fundamentally change averse, in denial about the need for new directions, or so wedded to the past that it cannot adapt to major changes such as becoming coeducational, discontinuing time-honored programs, or merging with a stronger institution. A *change-averse* board will listen attentively to the critics of change and usually undercut the president at the first sign of opposition. A *change-prone* board is as much of an obstacle to lasting change as one that is merely change averse. This overeager, hyperactive board seeks change too quickly, or veers erratically from one initiative to another, or wants to manage change rather than work with the president in bringing it about. The president with a change-prone board will find himself spending too much time toning down the board's initiative de jour to pursue a longer-term agenda.

The *change-adept* board represents the golden mean embodying the best features of those leery of change and those embracing it too quickly and too often. Such a board is prudent about engaging in change, insisting on quantifiable evidence that a new order is required before moving ahead. A board sophisticated about change takes pains to become knowledgeable about trends in higher education, understands the competitive posture of the institution it governs, and includes members with formal knowledge of change strategies and experience in leading change in complex organizations.

While the change-adept board is an ideal, it is an archetype many of the boards described in this book aspire to and several achieve. Many boards, however, are probably best characterized as *change-compliant*. They are patient with less-than-exceptional performance, usually defer to a dominant president, and on balance prefer to avoid conflict. But this type of board, while far from perfect, may provide reasonable support for presidential initiatives, given plenty of nurturing and frequent reminders of their duty to preserve and strengthen the institution. Individual members of a compliant board often provide sensible feedback in the "thinking out loud" discussions that should precede major change, may dutifully stand behind the president in the face of pushback, and serve adequately to support change that the president leads.

Some presidents prefer an overly accommodating board, believing it gives them more latitude in determining institutional direction. Ironically, executives whose boards have a compliant or even submissive personality often complain that their board members are not fully engaged in the work of the board or the institution. Suffice it to say that an able president with a compliant board can get some good things done. Much more can be accomplished, however, when an able president partners with a talented group of board members committed to the work of change.

The board in our hypothetical case seems to have hovered between the change-averse board and the compliant board that agrees to change as long as it does not upset the campus or alumni too much. This board allowed the former president to serve beyond the point of peak effectiveness and apparently failed to learn the challenges that the institution faced or the remedies available to it. Had the president devoted more attention to educating board members on both scores and enlisting their support in his change plans, he might have enjoyed more success, even with this ambivalent group.

Sustaining Board Enthusiasm for Change

Once we ironed out our respective leadership responsibilities in a retreat, the board backed away from their operational role and let me lead—not just run— the place… The new normal requires an actively engaged board. The corporate executives on the board have high expectations of chief executive officers, and they appreciate the stresses on those executives.

—JAMES C. VOTRUBA, president, Northern Kentucky University

Attentiveness to the board's interest and role in change is especially important when the president initiates the change and makes the case for his approach with board members, some of whom may be quietly skeptical. Here are some suggestions for keeping the board informed, engaged, and supportive of change as it unfolds.

1. Develop a sense of shared purpose well before embarking on a plan for change—for example, restoring financial health, making the institution more competitive overall, strengthening its educational effectiveness, or improving graduation rates. This purpose, and the eventual plans to achieve it, provides a structure for the board-president relationship that is much more positive than merely "getting along." Present change as being about building a stronger, more sustainable, and higher-performing institution, not about fulfilling the president's vision. This attitude will help ensure that the change agenda persists even after a president departs. At Northwest Health Sciences University, the board continues to scrutinize and discuss the shift to an integrated model for class and clinical experiences that encompasses both allopathic and homeopathic methods. No one forgets that this model lies at the core of the university's change agenda.

2. Confirm buy-in from the board with unequivocal statements of support from board leadership and a majority of members. The chair should take responsibility for ensuring that the board owns the plan for change every bit as much as the president does. Seeking the board's formal endorsement of the plan at the start, and at significant milestones along the way, will help force skeptics or naysayers to voice their concerns and enable change advocates to address them. Before Metro State went ahead with its new master level programs, the board chair made sure that board members who harbored serious reservations were heard and eventually persuaded of the logic behind the change.

3. Educate the board, perhaps with the help of outside experts, on the art of change, including the likely challenges it will confront during the process. Remind board members that significant change invites pushback and criticism, that the board itself may become the target of complaint, and that they need to support both the change agenda and the president in the face of opposition. The University of Dubuque holds annual educational seminars that include the board, the president, senior university staff, and often external experts. These gatherings keep discussions of the institution's

change trajectory and modifications to it front and center in the board's consciousness.

4. Engage the board in discussions of progress on the change agenda at every board meeting, report regularly on advancements, and devote substantive portions of board retreats to thinking out loud about all important aspects of the change process. Communicate between meetings, as well, on the progress of change with the chair, board leaders, and as many members as possible. Seek the advice of those who have something to offer as well as those who believe they do. Virtually all the institutions studied follow that practice, usually to a high degree. Busy board members and those with multiple interests can become inattentive to the change agenda unless the chair and the president work together to bring their focus back to the changes at hand.

5. Celebrate success along the way, and recognize important milestones as well as the responsible faculty and staff. Confirm achievements as they occur. Rather than exclude staff members from board meetings or minimize their conversations with board members, most institutions highlighted in this book encourage interaction among the board and the staff and faculty members who are carrying out the change. This practice has the double benefit of keeping board members well informed and enabling them to recognize the accomplishments of faculty and staff members with real knowledge of what they have done—instead of the more usual pro forma congratulations.

Learning to Lead Change

The task of changing oneself, of adjusting or accommodating one's personality and preferred way of communicating and interacting with others, presents subtle challenges. Character is destiny, according to Greek dramatists, who believed that immutable personality traits determined one's fate. Behavior, though shaped by genetics, prior learning, and environment, can be adjusted to yield more-effective habits of change leadership if the president is willing to learn more about himself. An important but often-ignored step in the change process is rigorous self-evaluation that enables the president to modify personal behavior and work in tandem with a team, sometimes including board members, to complete the leadership portfolio. This work is especially important for presidents nurtured in the academy, who missed out on the leadership-development opportunities available to upwardly mobile executives in the business sector and to senior officers in the military.

The presidents interviewed for this book share certain change-leadership traits, outlined here to help other presidents get a more precise fix on their own leadership characteristics. The willingness to confront one's strengths and weaknesses as a change leader takes emotional courage, to be sure. But then so does leading change in difficult circumstances.

> *There is no substitute for an active, personally committed CEO who is willing to do the critical things that only a CEO can do during periods of change.*
>
> —DAVID NADLER, *Champions of Change: How CEOs and Their Companies are Mastering the Skills of Radical Change* (Jossey-Bass, 1998)

Traits of Change Leaders

The characteristics that are most conducive to bringing about positive change include an ability to connect with others that is balanced by the strength of personality to make tough decisions—to do what needs to be done even if it means disappointing or angering others. The qualities that enable adroit presidents to work effectively with campus interests and personalities also serve them well in collaborating with board members on change.

Figure 5.1 Functional and Dysfunctional Change Behaviors by Presidents

MORE FUNCTIONAL TRAITS	LESS FUNCTIONAL TRAITS
• Open-mindedness in learning the institution's needs for change and the board's perceptions	• Reliance on solutions that have worked elsewhere instead of creative solutions that fit the current situation
• Skill in articulating a vision or strategic direction that recognizes the institution's values and inspires participation by the board and other stakeholders	• Tendency to focus on isolated problems rather than address problems in the context of a broad vision for change that the board embraces
• Ability to work with boards, faculty and staff, and community members in a participatory change mode	• Preference for being the sole author of the best ideas when it comes to leading change
• Capacity to express sincere respect for others engaged in the dialogue surrounding change, whether in support of or in opposition to it	• A strong-minded personality that, while decisive, fails to elicit support or wholehearted participation from board members and others
• Strength of character to make decisions, set boundaries, say no to proposals inconsistent with the change plan, and respectfully challenge a board on change issues	• Excessive desire to please others and to court the favor of the board or strong-willed members
• Personal resiliency and persistence in the face of pushback, criticism, unexpected obstacles, and instances when change does not seem to be progressing as planned	• Lack of persistence and difficulty maintaining focus when the pursuit of goals is an uphill struggle

The Work of Self-Appraisal

Acknowledging one's own strengths requires setting aside false or genuine modesty and relying on a trusted confidant to witness, expand, or temper the list. But it is much more difficult to identify the internal barriers to successful change leadership, especially weaknesses that we are embarrassed to acknowledge. An exercise associated with the venerable Johari Window is often used in business settings and with personal-growth groups to help participants come to know themselves better. With some modification, it is highly relevant to preparing to lead change at colleges and universities.

The Johari Window (its name combines the first names of its inventors, Joseph Luft and Harry Ingham) is made up of four quadrants, or "rooms," that hold space for aspects of one's personality as you and others perceive them: (1) traits known to the subject and to others; (2) traits recognized by others, but not the subject; (3) traits known to the subject, but invisible to others; and (4) deeply hidden traits available to neither the subject nor others (Figure 5.2).

In our variation on the original Johari exercise, the subject chooses five or six change-leadership traits from the traits listed above (or a list of their own making) and assigns them to three of the four quadrants. Their trusted colleagues—including, if possible, a few board members—do the same. The fourth quadrant (deeply hidden traits) can be ignored. The results work as a springboard to discussion of the leader's strengths and deficiencies when it comes to change. If the environment for this work is safe and without threat of retaliation, the discussion can be extremely useful to the leader and the team. The exercise does require a leader with the maturity to recognize his faults and confront them in the presence of others. A less-threatening approach to increasing self-awareness involves using the Johari Window to highlight the importance of acknowledging quadrant 2 and 3 traits. This exercise promotes discussion of the change capacities of a team without assigning traits to any individual.

In our hypothetical case, neither the new president nor the board were aware of the counterproductive traits harbored by the other. The president apparently imagined positive qualities in the board that did not exist, and he was blind to his own impetuosity, impatience, and inability to listen. This narrative did not need to end badly. The president appears to have been smart, creative, and energetic. The board did not understand the dynamics of change, but it genuinely wanted a stronger institution. If the president had been more alert to the culture of the campus and the need to prepare for change, if he had partnered with the board in building its comprehension of change, and if he had been more insightful about his own leadership style, this tale might have been a success story.

Figure 5.2 Johari Window: Leadership Self-Appraisal

	Known to Self	Not Known to Self
Known to Others	Quadrant 1 Public Self/Arena	Quadrant 2 Blind Spots
Not Known to Others	Quadrant 3 Hidden Facade	Quadrant 4 Unconscious Self/Unknown

Any leader in the public spotlight—especially a college president pursuing a highly visible change agenda—will find it challenging to come across as humble enough to admit mistakes and make adjustments in strategy and personal style. Doing so demands emotional maturity, as well as a touch of theater. Too much diffidence, and the community loses confidence in the leader; too little self-deprecation, and the leader appears arrogant. One especially able president in our study regularly asks senior staff to bring the bad news first—including news that is critical of the president's own decisions—and assures them there is no penalty for honesty. Several other presidents periodically engage in a "mutual expectations" conversation with their boards. Off the record in executive session with a facilitator, each party asks the other, "What should I/we consider changing in our communications with you in order to help move this institution forward?" As one president put it, "This candid conversation helps keep little issues from becoming major wedges between the board and the president. Both sides agree to adjust their behavior a bit to accommodate the other. We feel more comfortable with each other afterwards."

Developing Plans for Change

If the strategic plan and the budget were dependent variables, the board was the independent variable. They understood that a new plan was needed because of the work they did to understand governance. Now, they have a remarkable tool—the strategic plan—to hold me and the institution accountable.
—NEIL KERWIN, President, American University

Savvy change planners are sensitive to the point-counterpoint in the music of change: that is, the interplay of emotional reactions to change and the more linear, objective dimension that focuses on the product of change. Ronald A. Heifetz's work on the role of change leaders in enabling the community to adapt itself to often unwelcome and uncomfortable change, summarized in Chapter 2, represents the human side of the change equation. John P. Kotter's eight-step change process, referred to in Chapter 4, draws attention to the more linear dimension, which moves confidently from establishing a sense of urgency and a new vision to anchoring new approaches at the conclusion of the process. The point is that presidents and boards need to discuss how they will orchestrate both aspects of change at their institution, with its internal politics, values, and personalities on the one hand and the more objective need to achieve measurable results on the other.

The board of a large public university ignored the human realities surrounding change and the independent-mindedness of the faculty senate when it insisted that the president bring strategic change in fairly short order. What it got was a no-confidence vote in the board and president, but precious little strategic movement. By contrast, both Roosevelt and Metro State take great pains to ensure alignment among board strategic goals, institutional strategies, and the work of the campus. Roosevelt's board discusses strategic directions at length and approves no initiative that the institution's strategic goals do not support. Whether it is a new graduate program, the Hotel and Hospitality Learning Center, or a controversial pay-for-performance plan, no major initiative moves forward at Metro State without a high level of concurrence among the board, the president, and the campus. The dynamic nature of both institutions confirms that securing this alignment does not impede change, but rather helps ensure its success.

Two Board-President Change Partnerships
Roosevelt University • Metropolitan State College of Denver

Founded as the equal-opportunity Thomas Jefferson College in 1945, Roosevelt University has long maintained a deep commitment to social justice and access to university education that sets it apart from many other independent universities. Since 2002, with Charles R. Middleton as president, Roosevelt has stayed true to its progressive traditions while strengthening the curriculum and seeking greater stature. *U.S. News & World Report* ranks Roosevelt as the second-most-diverse private university in the Midwest. Incoming student test scores are rising, as is the number of doctoral-qualified faculty. A signature $129-million building in Chicago's downtown Loop is a symbol of Roosevelt's new mission, its positive future, and its institutional turnaround.

Founded in 1965 as an associate-degree-granting institution, Metropolitan State College of Denver was intended as a low-cost, high-access college. Two years later, Metro State was authorized to begin offering baccalaureate degrees. In 1973, the Auraria Higher Education Center was built, and Metro State joined the Community College of Denver and the University of Colorado at Denver on the tri-institutional downtown campus. When Colorado's governor removed Metro State from a four-campus governing system and created a separate governing board in 2002, the college took on renewed vitality and higher aspirations. After a two-year search, the board hired Colorado native Steve Jordan as president. Working in close partnership, the board and Jordan have aimed to make Metro State the preeminent public urban baccalaureate institution in the nation.

(For more on change at Roosevelt University and Metropolitan State College of Denver, see Appendix.)

Lessons for Presidents to Consider

Use committees and board expertise appropriately to vet strategic issues and advance strategic initiatives.

Productive, meaningful, engaging committees are especially important for large boards because they give board members a smaller group in which their expertise and perspectives can be heard and they can make a difference. At Roosevelt, the 60-member board once filtered all committee recommendations through an executive committee, which had to approve them before they were submitted for full board discussion and vote. Now all of the board's committees make recommendations directly to the full board. Much of the board's work is done in a series of committee meetings held in the three weeks leading up to each board meeting. Committees address strategic issues—for example, a board resolution to shift from having 40 percent of the credit hours generated by full-time faculty to a schedule of courses in which 60 percent of the credit hours are to be taught by this group as an important academic-quality measure.

At Metro State, a much smaller board of nine members applies the talents of individual trustees to college initiatives. For example, board members with experience in urban development, human resources, and the regional political scene work with the president in advancing programs like the Hotel and Hospitality Learning Center, which required public-private cooperation and support from the city of Denver.

Be intentional and strategic about board composition and board development.

The clarity of mission and strategies at Roosevelt changed board and institutional dynamics. Chuck Middleton has been intentional about cultivating the board, which is especially important because of its large size. The board works hard to define and adhere to appropriate governance roles. During meetings, board members gently call each other out about getting into the weeds. The executive committee has evolved from a strong decision-making body to a sounding board. Attendance at full board meetings is exceptional.

As a public institution, Metro State has a board nominated by the governor. Nevertheless, the board has developed a culture that prizes participation, board development, and self-scrutiny. All board members participate in rigorous evaluation of new initiatives—whether proposed by the board (such as the pay-for-performance program), jointly by the board and the president (such as the Hotel and Hospitality Learning Center), or by the president alone (such as the new graduate program). The board is also scrupulous about engaging external reviewers to help it assess its own performance and that of the president.

Set clear, quantifiable strategic objectives.

With leadership from a new president, Roosevelt developed a strategic plan. Today, both the board and the university are grounded in strategic goals, and that is a fundamental change. The board has adopted a purposeful approach to mission, image, metrics, and growth. The university's strategic objectives, developed in 2003, are intentionally broad concepts, not action plans. The board uses them routinely to place decisions and initiatives in context. Every board action and major discussion is explicitly tied to one or more goals.

Chuck Middleton's approach has been to consolidate gains and move forward systematically. He believes strongly in the board making decisions step by step, gaining comfort and confidence along the way. As the pace of change escalates, the magnitude of the decisions rises. Once, the board agonized over spending $35 million to join a residence-hall consortium. More recently, and after an extended series of discussions, the board unanimously and swiftly approved a $185-million bond issue (tripling the university's debt load) using $129 million to build the university's signature 32-story building.

The robust culture of decision making within Metro State's board features much back-and-forth between the president and the board before they reach agreement on the path forward. In one example, Steve Jordan made the case to the board that increasing student retention demanded a larger cadre of full-time faculty to provide support for the institution's many first-generation students. Ultimately, the board supported his proposal, on the condition that he present metrics showing the impact of additional faculty on retention. Jordan supplied the numbers, which confirmed his view.

Recognize that the presidency will always be a work in progress.

As a radically new environment emerges, veteran and novice presidents need to do some soul searching to ask if their most fundamental and personal ways of leading need to be adjusted to the times. An exercise like the Johari Window can be very helpful in this work of introspection and personal growth.

Topics for Board and President Discussion

1. ***Flawed relationships.*** Discuss the hypothetical example in this chapter or another instructive tale of ineffective relationships between boards and presidents. Do you agree with the analysis in this chapter? What are other ways of explaining the unfortunate turn of events? What can be done to salvage the relationship and the change agenda?

2. ***Attitude toward change.*** Discuss your college's or university's attitude toward change in general and the kind of change the board and president believe should be considered. Review the attitudes, as you understand them, of faculty, alumni, legislators, the public, and other stakeholder groups. What strategies are available for communicating with these groups and persuading them to understand and perhaps participate in change?

3. ***Board readiness.*** How well informed and unified is your board when it comes to change? Discuss board organization—committee structure and assignments, the agenda-setting process, the time devoted to change discussions during and between meetings—to learn more about change in general, specific changes that should be considered, and the board's potential contribution.

4. ***President's strengths.*** Encourage the president to appraise his or her own talents for change leadership. What special strengths does he or she bring to the table? What kind of support does he or she need from the board to bring about the desired changes? Where does he or she need a strong senior staff to "complete" his or her leadership?

5. ***Successes and roadblocks.*** Discuss planning that takes into account the quantifiable measures of success that will define what actually changes as well as the likely roadblocks to change. Applying the law of thirds (in many change situations, roughly one-third of the people involved will support it, one-third will oppose it, and the rest are apt to be indifferent), how will the board and the president accommodate each faction? When the unavoidable pushback erupts, what form will it likely take? How will the board and the president respond?

Chapter 6

BUILDING THE CHANGE-ADEPT BOARD

When trustees are asked, "Why do you take the time to serve on this board?" The answers are remarkably consistent. Board members say that they want to strengthen and sustain the institution. If they serve on the board of a public university or system, they emphasize its importance to the economic and social development of the state or region. Especially for alumni, the notion of giving back to ensure that a younger generation enjoys the benefits of a college degree figures prominently in their motivations.

The notion of changing the institution to sustain its vitality and enable it to deliver individual and communal benefits is seldom mentioned in these introductory discussions. But before long, the substance of change—if not the actual word itself—enters the conversation. After all, change is not an end in itself, but a way of moving the institution and often the board to a better position. Every board and president that AGB studied engaged in a change agenda that ameliorated at-risk characteristics or advanced the institution to higher levels of quality, reputation, and financial strength—or both. They could not have succeeded without a change-adept board.

This chapter explores the use of strategic recruitment and education to develop a board that is proficient at the kind of change its institution needs. Creating a change-adept board is much like sailing a boat. The boat needs to float, and it needs to tack to its destination port. Keeping the institution afloat—in finances, facilities, compliance, risk oversight, educational quality, fund raising, and so on—is the board's fundamental fiduciary or stewardship responsibility. If the board falls short on any of these tasks, the boat could take on water, and it might even sink. This fundamental board work is so essential, say Richard Chait and his colleagues, that "most nonprofit trustees and executives consider it synonymous with trusteeship." [8]

Intentionally building a change-adept board adds a dimension to this traditional model. Creating a board equipped to lead and contribute to change is much like using the right navigation skills to guide a boat safely toward port. A change-adept board requires new board members who are experienced with change, an educational process to prepare board members for their role in change, and regular evaluation of the board's capacity to improve itself and the institution.

....
[8] Chait et al., *Governance as Leadership*, p. 33.

In pursuit of this richer concept of board development, this chapter addresses three interrelated questions:

- What strategic recruitment practices attract board members who are skilled at leading change?
- What approaches to board education and development help build a change-adept board?
- How should a board assess its capacity to engage in change?

A surprising number of the institutions that AGB studied developed stronger boards before the crisis or other change driver occurred. This chapter looks especially to the models of Tulane University and Johnson & Wales University. At Tulane, board members and the president successfully rebuilt a board with broader leadership experience seven years before Hurricane Katrina left the campus five feet underwater. Leadership from this change-adept board and its able president, Scott S. Cowen, is the reason Tulane has prospered since Katrina while some other institutions in the region remain in recovery mode. At Johnson & Wales, the board chair established a committee of trustees to reinvent the way the board did business. This new board, which included some veteran members, launched a strategic redirection toward higher levels of quality in educating and graduating students.

Characteristics of a Change-Adept Board

Virtually all the boards AGB studied are working to become more adept at change, although some are close to that Holy Grail and others are at earlier points in the journey. A genuinely change-adept board combines the right experience in its members, exceptional leadership from its chair, a mature relationship with the president, and the intangible qualities of insight and good judgment applied to its role in the change process. Such characteristics, gleaned from observing the boards described in this book, equip a board to contribute to change. Members of these boards:

- Have the right expertise for the institution's strategic pursuits;
- Display exceptional personal commitment to the institution and their board work;
- Are independent-minded but act as a team with a common goal;
- Consider board service a higher calling;
- Understand the nature of governance and achieve the right balance with the president in working for change;
- Match their work to the institution's current stage in the change process and the kind of change it requires; and
- Remain open and flexible in their thinking about what the institution needs and their role in helping bring about the change.

The schema for building a board with these qualities assumes traditional standards of board selection and development, but it goes further to emphasize the skills a board needs to engage in positive change. The model has three components (Figure 6.1): strategic recruitment of experienced change leaders to the board; development of the board's capacity to lead change in the institution; and evaluation of the board's interest in and potential for change leadership (Figure 6.1). All three elements are required for an effective board-building strategy: The right new members rejuvenate the board; continuing development improves board performance; and self-assessment clarifies what the board needs in terms of new members and board education.

Figure 6.1 Building the Change-Adept Board

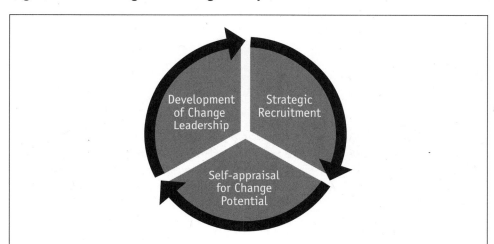

Strategic Recruitment

The earnest president of a small liberal arts college asked experienced colleagues to recommend some good potential board members—a distressing approach to board recruitment and not just because it was so haphazard. The request suggested that the board was shirking its responsibility to work with the president on systematic recruitment. Ironically, the college had a compelling story to tell, the president needed a strong board committed to realizing its potential, and board membership during this time of change would have been an especially meaningful experience.

The board's obligation to ensure exceptional talent in succeeding generations of its members is as serious as recruiting the right president. Board recruitment requires a collaborative approach, with the president, the board governance or nominating committee, and the executive committee all actively involved. An essential building block of a great board is the time spent assembling a comprehensive board matrix including skill sets that support change, developing a list of potential members, and scripting a compelling pitch to prospects.

Great expectations lead to high performance. It is a mistake to minimize the time and energy expected of board members just to make it is easier to persuade busy people to join. The highest-functioning boards target individuals who have strengths to contribute, are inspired by the institution's change trajectory, and are willing to devote considerable time to board work. When recruiting new members, these boards do everything in their power to convince strong prospects to say yes. They make it clear that board service requires every member's best thinking, along with a significant time commitment. They deal frankly with the issue of monetary contributions, stating explicitly that the institution should be among a board member's top three giving priorities—and ideally number one or two.

Forming New Recruitment Habits

On many boards, members' skills and attitudes are misaligned with the institution's need for change. The fissure between the board's qualifications and the capacity to bring positive change is not intentional, but it is rather the result of three mutually reinforcing habits: keeping board members on for too long, seeking a balanced roster rather than a change-adept one, and living with steep learning curves characterized by having lots to learn but too little time for the task.

> *The board looks for out-of-the-box solutions to our challenges … The board is continually renewing a start-up mentality among the trustees. We seek new trustees who are alumni, which is very important to this board, and who are proactive, not afraid of change, and committed to success.*
> —KELLY O'DEA, Board Chair, Thunderbird School of Global Management

Recruiting for a Change-Adept Board

Although a few boards still have arbitrary recruiting practices that lack clear intention, most begin by analyzing gaps in board talents and skill sets and then seek to fill those gaps with new members. This best practice leads to a balanced board composed of the usual array of backgrounds, including business (especially finance), law, health care, nonprofits, and higher education. Board balance also encompasses varying degrees of wealth and generosity. To promote board vitality and leadership succession, the best governance committees also seek board members with less tangible but essential skills, such as leadership, independent mindedness, creativity, and interpersonal communications talent.

Today's competitive and constantly changing environment requires expanded recruiting techniques that identify these qualities in potential board members. People who have contributed to positive change in complex organizations are good prospects because they are likely to be adaptable and ready to contribute to change when it is needed. The same goes for current or former academic leaders who have a track record of moving their institutions forward relative to their competition.

Tulane's board experienced a dramatic makeover under the leadership of President Cowen and two board members—alumnus John Koerner and Tulane parent Martin

Payson. Some of the important changes included reducing the board terms from 15 to 12 years, increasing the board size from 25 to 35, adding more national members to reflect the university's plan to attract a more geographically diverse student body, instituting board assessment on a three-year schedule, establishing written expectations for board members, including their financial commitment, and designing a formal orientation program for new members and ongoing education for all members.

Johnson & Wales had transitioned from a proprietary institution to a private, nonprofit some years earlier, but there was less change in board membership. The board still consisted largely of friends and associates of the institution's one-time owners. Chair (and former president) John Yena and a board committee spearheaded the transformation of Johnson & Wales' board processes. The changes included the introduction of term limits, board-member assessment, orientation for new members, a special provision for former board members to become "legacy members," and board-recruitment strategies based on institutional directions rather than personal relationships.

There are plenty of cautionary tales of well-intentioned board members, often those impatient with the fragmented power structure of the academy, who create more problems than positive change. With luck, several players from an existing team roster will display the skill and knowledge to contribute to change. If not, an expanded recruitment matrix should include traits that underpin change leadership. These skill sets are also important to high-functioning governance, whatever the change environment:

- Knowledge of global trends and directions in higher education;
- Familiarity with the league of peer institutions that the institution competes with or may want to join;
- Background in competing institutions and segments, including the fast-growing accredited proprietary sector;
- Formal knowledge and experience with the art and science of organizational change; and
- Experience at the executive level with change in business and nonprofit enterprises.

Shortening Lead Times and Accelerating Turnover

Several years may elapse before even quick learners on the board absorb enough knowledge of the institution, the industry, and the board to make positive contributions. There are several reasons for this extended learning curve. Too many board-education programs suffer from too much, or too little, information. New board members may be advised to sit quietly through a few meetings until they get to know the territory, so a year or more may pass before they really take the field. At the other extreme, more than one board member confronted with a six-inch-thick board briefing book has likened the process to "drinking from a fire hose." The best board-education programs, like those at Tulane, Johnson & Wales, and others, provide a digestible overview of the institution but also address the challenges and change issues it confronts. New trustees are introduced quickly to the change trajectory and the work of the board in building a stronger institution, and board development is viewed as a continuous process that occurs throughout a trustee's tenure.

Low board turnover represents a mixed blessing at best. To be sure, institutional memory is an important asset, but so are fresh perspectives and energy. Certain practices combine to keep too many underperforming board members at the table for too long: the lack of meaningful board-member evaluation (and little connection between evaluation and reappointment), the absence of term limits, and the tendency to ignore term limits where they exist.

Boards operating in a change environment need to accelerate the learning curve for new recruits and engineer equilibrium between enthusiastic new members and experienced veterans. Tulane University dealt with both concerns by instituting an aggressive board-education program for incoming and veteran members alike. The new chair at Widener University took a direct approach in encouraging long-serving board members who had become disengaged to retire or not seek reappointment. He suggested directly to underperforming and unengaged trustees that they change their level of commitment to the board or resign.

Focused Strategies that Attract Change Leaders

Corporate Talent

Leaders of complex businesses represent fertile ground as future board members and board chairs. Some academics decry the corporatization of boards. But on balance, such board members bring a much-needed set of talents to their governance work. The best corporate leaders respect clear objectives, appreciate well-selected metrics to assess progress, and think in terms of strategic alternatives and positioning in a competitive environment. They also work very hard for organizations and purposes they commit to and accept change as normal in today's competitive world. At critical turning points, the board member who has taken calculated business risks or turned around a major enterprise is often the first to step forward to spark an overdue change of direction at a college or university.

Change-adept board members from the corporate world quickly stepped up to the plate to reverse a precipitous enrollment and financial decline at Thunderbird School of Global Management, today a top-ranked institution. At Hendrix College, business leaders on the board knew from experience that forecasting followed by decisive action would support a change process in response to heightened competition and enrollment loss. Other scenarios might have led both institutions to recover, but the facts of each case point to the value of a business-savvy board.

Higher-Education Experts

One experienced university board member observed that a board without a higher-education professional would be like the General Motors board without directors who know about building cars. A current or former senior dean or a president from another institution can serve as translator for board colleagues from corporate backgrounds, helping them understand—if not fall in love with—the sacred texts, rituals, and taboos of academic culture.

But no one appreciates the self-styled expert who lectures the board on conventional academic practices. The provost of a liberal arts college joined the board of a professionally oriented university and predictably ascended to the chair of the academic affairs committee. He stoutly resisted suggestions that his committee review both the business plan and quality assurance measures for new programs, insisting that in "real universities" the academic affairs committee did not sully itself with commercial considerations. This board member never appreciated the ethos of the college he was supposed to govern and opposed any change agenda that did not mimic traditional academic practices.

Widener University made a far better choice by inviting Ira Harkavy, a nationally acknowledged leader in the civic-engagement movement, to join the board. As the founding director and associate vice president of the Netter Center for Community Partnerships at the University of Pennsylvania, Harkavy is well versed in what it takes to develop an applied approach to learning within a traditional academic milieu. He is an expert on change in the academic world, and as chair of Widener's civic-engagement committee, he enabled the board to align its structure with a top university priority.

Geographic Diversity with Added Benefits

Tulane's experience suggests that bringing national members onto a board provides more than geographic diversity. President Scott Cowen's predecessors never attended meetings of the nominating committee, but he suggested that he participate. That was a watershed moment, because board expansion had opened 10 new slots. Soon the nominating committee developed explicit criteria. As a result, all major U.S. metropolitan areas were represented, and new board members with experience as corporate and nonprofit directors joined. The board also became more philanthropic; fully one-third of the most recent campaign total, including several transformational-level gifts, came from board members. By going national in its search for new board members, Tulane availed itself of an expanded talent pool, moving beyond its base of bankers and lawyers to embrace entrepreneurs, philanthropists, and money managers. This group had the background and attitude to join Scott Cowen in moving Tulane from a regionally respected institution to one of national prominence.

National board members can also bring valuable diversity to public universities. The Ohio University board is empowered to select "national trustees," nonvoting members who live beyond the borders of the Buckeye State. A team including the president vets potential national trustees, all of whom have accepted the university's invitation. This flexibility brings special expertise to the board, as a recent selection of a national expert in information technology attests. At the time, the university was making substantial investments in its information systems. The new board member gave the administration helpful advice on that process and reassured the rest of the board in an area of high cost where few shared his level of experience. Other public universities should explore this option for diversifying their boards because it can bring both a national perspective and special expertise not available in a strictly local or state-bounded board.

"Just In Time" Board Members

Beginning a major initiative without substantial, relevant board experience is like driving blindfolded. Institutions facing major change should be ready to make exceptions to rules about term length, term limits, and board size so they can appoint new board members who possess distinct change-leadership strengths. An institution considering a major international initiative with board members inexperienced in international higher education or business needs to recruit people with this expertise. The same applies to any major change: an operational turnaround, the acquisition of a major program such as a law or dental school, recovery from a disaster such as a fire or flood, or the launch of a new delivery system such as online degree programs. In today's competitive world of higher education, boards need to be able to recruit and appoint new members with the right expertise much more quickly than they often do.

Recruiting Trustees for Public Institutions

Board members in public colleges and universities are sometimes thought to be less effective than their counterparts in private institutions because their selection process is political. But this belief is questionable. Presidents and board members exert more influence over the choice of new members than is commonly understood. Almost 70 percent of the presidents of public college and universities in the AGB 2010 survey of governing boards say they have "some or considerable influence"[9] over board selection.

Many governors and their staffs will heed board requests for new members with particular skills in, say, finance or audit, even if they reserve the right to select an individual of their own choosing. With higher-education reform—improving retention and graduation rates, producing more graduates in STEM disciplines, applying university research to economic growth—a prominent goal in many states (see Chapter 1), governors may be encouraged to select trustees who support this change agenda. In several instances, an influential board chair nearly always gets the members the board wants, although the governor goes through a formal nominating process. Presidents and public board members who work with their governors to secure the most-able members are more likely to succeed in attracting the change-oriented leaders they seek. Tom Davis, board secretary at Ohio University, reports that the board is batting .500 when it comes to nominating top-priority board members. He adds that other appointments have brought valued skills as well.

....

[9] *Policies, Practices, and Composition of Governing Boards of Public Colleges and Universities* (AGB Press, 2010).

Developing the Change-Adept Board

If the job of strategic board recruitment is getting the right people on the bus, to use Jim Collins' phrase, then the function of board education and development is making sure the passengers work effectively together. Becoming a change-adept board means redesigning conventional board-development programs, which usually take two complementary approaches.

The first approach—reinforcing the board's fiduciary role—involves addressing topics such as avoiding conflicts of interest or the appearance thereof, maintaining the management independence of the sort required of publicly held corporations by the Sarbanes-Oxley Act, and complying with state and federal regulations for good-faith governance. The second approach—improving how the group operates as a social organism based on canonized best practices—involves the interactive processes that a particular board employs to arrive at sound decisions. Those touch on how meeting agendas are set; the importance of using consent agendas to free up time for policy discussions; the role and assignment of committees; the kind and timeliness of information provided to the board; the role of the chair; and rules of engagement clarifying how board members communicate with each other, the president, and the staff.

The two approaches, often combined in a workshop or retreat setting, are fundamental to effective board development and responsible governance. But to prepare boards to assert change leadership, both approaches must be expanded, and a third approach—understanding the art of change—should be added.

A pyramid is a useful form for describing how a well-planned development program equips board members for change. According to Euclidian geometry, a pyramid has three or more triangular sides converging to a point. At the point of convergence is a board prepared to effect positive change. The three faces of the pyramid are an expanded understanding of the fiduciary role; group processes that encourage board members to think in a fresh way about their institution's need for change; and greater appreciation of change techniques and the board's role in it (Figure 6.2).

Figure 6.2 The Board-Development Pyramid

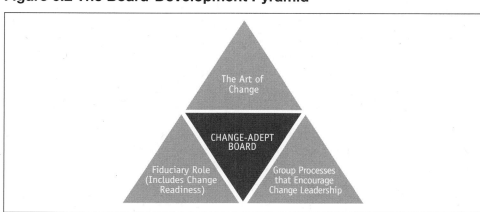

Change as Part of Fiduciary Responsibility

The legal term *fiduciary* refers to one who holds assets in trust for the benefit of another. The fiduciary places the beneficiary's interests first and acts in accordance with that priority. Out of this concept grows the notion that college and university boards hold the institution they govern in trust for society, for the university community, and, especially in the case of publicly supported institutions, for the people of the state. Historically and to this day, fiduciary responsibility implies acting prudently. Often, change is the only prudent course. As Hendrix College faced threats to its finances and its ability to attract top students, one board member asserted that "not changing represented the greatest risk." Another added that the board "needed to change the school to preserve the institution we love."

Board fiduciary responsibility—the first goal of board development—rests on three pillars whose interpretation undergoes constant expansion:

- The duty of loyalty;
- The duty of care; and
- The duty of obedience.

A logical corollary to this list is the responsibility to ensure that, when change is required to sustain the institution, the right change occurs. By the same token, neglecting to make change in a timely way for whatever reason may violate the duty to act in good faith. In a competitive environment that may threaten an institution's quality and sometimes its survival, exercising fiduciary responsibility may take a proactive turn. The duty to change would involve being alert to the warning signs that change is needed, actively seeking evidence of institutional quality and insisting on change where quality is lacking, and reviewing forecasts of financial and other trends so the board and administration address problems before they morph into crises. Taking steps to build a stronger board—as Tulane did well before Katrina, as Hendrix did well before September 11, and as Johnson & Wales did well before the worldwide economic downturn—exemplifies sound fiduciary behavior.

To be sure, board education on fiduciary duties should emphasize the legal requirement to act in the interest of beneficiaries and to preserve tangible assets. Neglecting to assure proper financial accounting, independent audit reviews, or responsible maintenance of the physical plant and failing to avoid both the appearance and the reality of conflict of interest are serious breaches. But board development should also address the proactive side of fiduciary responsibility: the need to bring change when change is the prudent thing to do.

At this writing, the board of a respected college (not part of AGB's research) is patiently awaiting a turnaround promised by the president while the unrestricted endowment declines by millions each year. This women's college in the mid-Atlantic attracted daughters of the middle class to a safe campus with a mild socially progressive ethos. As the pool of students interested in single-sex education declined, the college shifted its attention to educating lower-income students, many of whom are women of color, who could not afford the costly tuition. Steep tuition discounting followed, as did annual deficits. With the current business model, the college will be up for sale or closure within a few years. No one would argue that these board members are exercising their fiduciary responsibility, especially when there are successful examples of independent colleges with high-access missions. This institution is merely an extreme illustration of fiduciary failure that is becoming more common as competition for students, resources, and reputation intensifies.

> *[Board] members develop mutual respect; because they respect one another, they develop trust; because they trust one another, they share difficult information; because they all have the same, reasonably complete information, they can challenge one another's conclusions coherently; because a spirited give-and-take becomes the norm, they learn to adjust their own interpretations in response to intelligent questions.*
>
> --JEFFREY A. SONNENFELD, "What Makes Great Boards Great," *Harvard Business Review* (September 2002)

Board Processes Conducive to Change

Opening up the way the board operates as a group is the second important element in creating a change-adept board. Boards that are most open to constructive change exemplify robust, active social systems ready to engage with issues that matter. They interact with each other and the president around those issues as a socially mature group, and they are willing to challenge, ask tough questions, and debate the merits of various proposals while remaining cordial.

At American University, for example, board vice-chair Thomas A. Gottschalk (who had served as interim board chair) worked in close partnership with the new chair, Gary Abramson, to manage government and news-media inquiries and repair rifts within the board and between the board and the people on campus. This tandem arrangement, described as "board chair for the past, board chair for the future," repaired damage to the board and its reputation and also introduced more-transparent and inclusive governance practices.

Charles P. Morgan, who is credited with rebuilding the Hendrix College board in the years before it encountered competitive threats, cites embarrassingly low graduation rates as one hot-button issue the revitalized board adopted. The impetus for raising retention and graduation rates grew out of some friendly but intense conversations among board members and the president.

The environment in high-functioning, change-adept boards has these features:

- The board insists that information on the institution comes in clear, succinct formats.
- Metrics that matter are reported regularly to the board.

- "Thinking out loud" among board members and the president leads to better solutions.
- The chair encourages full participation in the debate.
- Meetings are robust conversations about important issues.
- Cordiality is prized, but so is constructive dissent.

Board chairs who recruit a higher performing caliber of board member emphasize the need to create a stimulating board environment. "These recruits joined us because I told them they would make a difference," one chair reported, "so I had to give them engaging, meaningful work." Independent-minded new board members will demand to be heard, and that is their great value to a board and institution facing major change. "The best board members question and challenge what you're doing," says Scott Cowen of Tulane. "But they also know that there's a point to move on. You would see that in our board meetings after Katrina: question, challenge, and base decisions on facts." Board development, whether facilitated by an outside expert or conducted by board members, should intentionally build these kinds of social behaviors into board deliberations if they do not exist. Coaching the board chair on the techniques of eliciting engagement from the board may be useful as well.

The Art of Change Leadership

Building a change-adept board requires adding a third component to board development: learning about the art of leading change. Becoming an adept student of change is as important for board members as knowing how to interpret the financial statements. This educative process requires studying models of change that have worked in social-sector organizations like colleges and universities; learning from presidents, board members, and others who have experienced success (and maybe failure) in real-life change efforts; and growing in wisdom from the experience of the change journey itself. Most often, the president is the executive agent of change, but the board must be an active partner in a process that always presents surprises along the way.

Learning about the board's role in leading change involves:

- Dialogue about change leadership as a fundamental board responsibility;
- Discussion of the literature of change;
- Attention to change models that fit corporate, social-sector, and academic organizations;
- A candid conversation between the board and the president about appropriate roles in bringing specific change; and
- Identification of the next steps in preparing for change leadership.

Figure 6.3 outlines some topics for augmenting the traditional board-development agenda when the goal is strengthening the board's capacity for change leadership.

Figure 6.3 Developing the Board's Capacity for Change

TOPIC FOR BOARD DEVELOPMENT	EXAMPLES FOCUSED ON CHANGE
Fiduciary Role	**Holding in trust may mean change.** • View change as sometimes a fiduciary responsibility and sometimes a requirement of stewardship. • Believe in the importance of "change to sustain." • Question the sustainability of current business models.
Group Process	**Robust dialogue yields better options.** • Hold open conversations about challenges and the need for change. • Encourage constructive dissent. • Invite frequent "thinking out loud" with the president. • Encourage all to participate. • Treasure open-mindedness.
Art of Change	**Prepare for change leadership.** • Discuss change as a board responsibility. • Study different change models. • Understand change in the academy. • Discuss with the president who does what in bringing change. • Promote continued learning as the change process moves forward.

Assessing Board Readiness for Change Leadership

Developing proficiency at any group task, especially one as complex as leading change, requires a candid appraisal of the group's abilities, commitment, and resources. Board members who contemplate playing a major role in institutional change have several choices when it comes to taking this inventory. The board can engage in a discussion of where they fall on the spectrum between change averse and change prone (see Chapter 4). A consultant can interview board members and perform a 360-degree evaluation of the group's preparedness to take on change leadership. Or, using the readiness assessment tool in Figure 6.4, the board can discuss critical questions to determine whether they are prepared to engage in major change. To encourage full participation, one or two trustees can act as thought leaders who frame and facilitate the discussion.

Figure 6.4 Change Readiness Assessment

1. Change and good governance

- Does the board believe that it can add value to the institution by playing a major role in a specific change?
- Is this role appropriate to sound governance?
- Is the change at hand really strategic or important enough to merit board involvement?
- Are we too eager to get involved in what are really operational issues that should be left to the president and his or her staff?
- How can the board become more engaged without sliding into micromanagement or eroding its objectivity?
- Are major issues of the institution's quality, reputation, or even continued existence at stake?
- Are we prepared to commit the time and energy to genuinely contribute to positive change over the long run?

2. Lessons from experience

- Has the board played a major role in bringing about change in the past? If not, why do we believe we should act this time? If we have contributed to change in the past, were our efforts successful and worth our time?
- What lessons could we draw from prior experience that would help us now?
- What would we do differently this time?

3. New learning

- What board members, presidents, and other experts could guide us based on their experience with change at institutions like ours?
- Are there books we should read? Conferences we should attend? Webinars we can participate in? Institutions we could visit to help us anticipate the pitfalls we might encounter?
- How will we measure success?
- In what ways should we adjust our board meeting format or agenda to facilitate this change work?
- What else can we do to educate ourselves on change and our role in bringing it about?

4. Working with the president

- How do we set the right boundaries between what the board should do and what the president should do?
- Are there some bright lines we should never cross?
- How can we support and challenge the president in this process?
- What does the president really think of our "help"?
- How can we work with the president to handle criticism and pushback during the change process?
- What is our role in communications, both on campus and in the community?

5. Engaging the faculty and others

- Do we agree that we need to work with faculty, staff, and students to bring about change? What roles would each play? Do we just listen? Actively seek their advice? Encourage their participation and grant a large measure of control?
- How do we work with the faculty without undercutting the president or our own authority as a board?
- How can we engage political and civic leaders, alumni, and others while maintaining our role as governors of this institution?
- Who else needs to feel a part of this change process for it to succeed?

Boards can use this set of questions in several ways. A list slimmed down to reflect the realities of a particular institution could be converted to an anonymous survey, with the results serving as a springboard for a conversation with the president. More-ambitious boards might retain an external facilitator to interview board members using the questions as a template and then conduct a board workshop on the findings. The simplest approach might be to ask a committee of veteran trustees to analyze board habits in light of these criteria and then lead a discussion with the whole board based on their conclusions.

Building Capacity through Board Self-Evaluation

Boards that conduct candid periodic self-evaluations and then act on the results usually contribute more to positive change than boards that tacitly assume they do not need to improve. But the focus of the evaluation is important too. Boards that measure themselves against standard good practices of governance—such as trustee attendance at meetings, sticking to policy setting rather than management, and listening to stakeholders—do better than those that eschew self-appraisal entirely. But these criteria tend to reinforce the status quo and enable some boards to believe that adequate performance is enough.

Probing self-evaluations that raise questions about the depth of the board's knowledge of the institution's competitive position, forecasts of the institution's likely financial position over the coming three to five years, and hard evidence of the real quality and effectiveness of its educational programs are more apt to provoke discussions of the need for change than the more reassuring surveys.

The Evolution of Two Change-Adept Boards
Tulane University • Johnson & Wales University

Both Tulane and Johnson & Wales illustrate the logical but sometimes overlooked reality that better boards with more effective processes make better decisions. In both cases, the building blocks for superior governance were broader board composition that reflected the institutions' strategic directions; improved board development and education; term-limit policies to replace veterans with new board members; and board self-assessment. When Hurricane Katrina hit, Tulane's board was up to the unprecedented challenge. Johnson & Wales' stronger board was positioned to challenge the institution's conventional thinking and insist on higher expectations for student retention and graduation.

(For more on change at Tulane University and Johnson & Wales University, see Appendix.)

Lessons for Building Change-Adept Boards

Focus the nominating process on alignment with the institution's strategic direction, not personal relationships with the president or board members.
Parallel to its transition from a proprietary school to a regionally accredited, nonprofit university, Johnson & Wales modified its governance structure so that a board member's professional performance and relationship to the institution's program and direction—not personal connections—determined board membership. This new governance model received high praise in accreditation and other external reports.

At Tulane, Scott Cowen became the first president to be a voting member of the board meetings. Cowen, a former business-school dean and author of a book on building a corporate board, had the credibility to bring about change at the board level. The board added 10 new positions, with Cowen helping to appoint members who would change the board's culture.

Set specific criteria, including an openness to positive change, in the process of recruiting new board members.
At Tulane, the nominating committee systematically defined the board's needs, including certain skill sets and geographic diversity. As a result, every major metropolitan area in the country is now represented on a board that had been

dominated by New Orleans–area residents. Board membership expanded from bankers and lawyers to include entrepreneurs, philanthropists, and money managers—people with the skills and attitudes that went beyond the desire to preserve a great institution to those that included changing it for the better. The entrepreneurs and business leaders come from an environment in which adaptability to changing circumstances is the norm.

Diversifying a board with new members requires diplomacy and compassion when it comes to saying goodbye to long-serving board members.

The change process at Johnson & Wales was traumatic for many board members, as expectations rose and people with years of service were asked to leave and become "legacy" members. A small committee—headed by respected board member and student of corporate governance Don Hubble and a consultant—interviewed every board member individually about the proposed changes and reported feedback to the chair. In several instances, Chair John Yena met with board veterans who were distressed over the prospect of losing their seats. After a robust conversation involving the entire board, the proposed changes were adopted, even though in a few instances long-standing relationships were fractured or terminated.

Look to advisory committees and similar groups as fertile ground for recruiting new board members.

Scott Cowen cultivates Tulane's President's Council, a national group of non-board-member advisors, as a training ground for future board members. After each board meeting, he presents the group with the same issues that the board has addressed to test and prepare potential successors for board service. These rehearsals help identify the most creative minds in the group, and they also generate fresh ideas for dealing with the university's challenges.

With its many advisory committees and close interactions with executives in program-related industries, Johnson & Wales enjoys numerous opportunities for observing potential board recruits. Much of this responsibility falls to the chair, although typically new members are known to several others on the board. JWU has also taken steps to attract several board members with substantive leadership experience in higher education.

Self-assessment is a prerequisite to building a more change-adept board.

A periodic (every two to three years), formal evaluation of the board's ability to contribute positively to change demands that a board be self-confident as well as a humbly committed to doing better. These assessments should include the board's own view of its performance, the perspective of an external reviewer, and a discussion of the gaps between the two. Both Tulane and Johnson & Wales actively conduct this kind of rigorous self-appraisal.

Topics for Board and President Discussion

1. ***Consensus on change.*** Have we discussed in some depth what it means for this board to become truly adept at change? Have we developed a high degree of consensus about and comfort with what we need to know as a board and the roles we can play in helping to bring change when it is needed?

2. ***Recruitment strategies.*** To what extent have we aligned our board recruitment strategies not only with our perennial needs for those versed in business, law, education, and so on, but also to meet the specific challenges facing our institution?

3. ***Identifying what the board needs.*** Have we identified the specific competencies we should seek among board members and discussed where we would find prospects?

4. ***Board learning on change.*** If we feel that we need to learn more about change in higher education, the kind of change our institution might require, and examples of successful board behavior at places like ours, what plans do we have to get that information? A workshop facilitated by some expert? Visits to other campuses? Discussions organized by board members or staff members?

5. ***Board-president partnership.*** Have we discussed and articulated fully the kind of working relationship we ought to have with our president, and has he or she been a full partner in that conversation? Do we regularly discuss with the president our expectations for each other when it comes to bringing positive change to our institution?

Chapter 7

MAKING A DIFFERENCE STATEWIDE: HOW SYSTEM BOARDS BRING CHANGE

Boards of the nation's more than 60 multicampus public systems share enormous responsibility and extraordinary potential to improve the educational experience of students, enable them to graduate more quickly with better credentials, and accelerate the application of university-based research to the economic and social needs of the nation. This work can measurably increase student's employability, income, and quality of life, and it better positions states to compete in a world where knowledge and knowledge workers are the essential strategic resource.

In 2008–2009, more than 12 million of the nation's 26.5 million students, or about 45 percent, enrolled in the more than 1,100 colleges and universities led by system boards, including community and technical colleges, historically black colleges and universities, multicampus entities, and major research universities (Figure 7.1). No other group of college or university board members has the potential to leverage positive change affecting the lives and careers of so many students. Yet if the possibilities are great, so are the challenges.

State governments created higher-education system boards to bring coherence and oversight to their public universities and colleges. Government leaders wanted to address public priorities seamlessly, reduce unproductive competition among institutions, realize more efficient use of state resources, and create a political and economic environment that would allow institutions of different sizes and missions to survive and fulfill their missions.

Although policy makers and the public sometimes are disappointed in the performance of system boards in accomplishing those occasionally contradictory goals, there is little question that systems are here to stay. As Aims C. McGuinness, a senior associate with the National Center for Higher Education Management Systems (NCHEMS), points out, they serve critical purposes that combine to ensure their continuation: the need to negotiate labor contracts centrally where collective bargaining exists; to capture scale economies in administering collective functions like joint purchasing and managing information technology; to maintain political equilibrium among competing interests and regions; and to present a single voice for higher education in the legislature. [10]

System boards once were expected to manage the proliferation and coordinate the efforts of higher-education institutions within a state. But now politicians and opinion makers call on such boards to expand access, accelerate progression from admissions to graduation, transform laboratory research into commercial products and processes, and meet the growing workforce needs of a high-tech environment with an aging population. Making this change in culture and mission, and taking specific steps to bring measurable change, is the topic of this chapter.

....
[10] Aims C. McGuinness, *A Model for Successful Restructuring in Higher Education: What Works and What Doesn't* (Jossey-Bass 1996).

Drawing especially on the experiences of three highly effective system boards—the University System of Maryland, the University of North Carolina System, and the University of Wisconsin System—this chapter explains the organization of state systems and explores the following questions:

- What heightened expectations for performance must system boards embrace?
- What new public policy mandates should they pursue?
- What barriers do system boards face as they strive to increase access, improve educational productivity, and raise the percentage of residents with two- and four-year degrees?
- What are the most powerful levers of change in multicampus systems?

How State Systems Work

Every state organizes higher-education governance differently. Richard Novak, senior vice president for programs and research at AGB, offers this explanation in his 2009 AGB white paper on system structures:

> A chief executive officer—usually called the system chancellor, system president, or commissioner—reports directly to a system board and manages a central administration office. He or she directly oversees the work of the institutional chief executives (presidents or chancellors). Often, the system head is the leading spokesperson for higher education in the state. Sometimes, he or she shares the stage with (and is sometimes eclipsed by) the president of the state's leading university and a state official responsible for higher education coordination.

> About half the states orchestrate public colleges and universities under statewide coordinating boards, while the rest rely on somewhat more potent governing boards (Figure 7.1). The terms coordinating and governing can be misleading. Some coordinating boards, such as West Virginia's, hold authority over missions, budgets, and even presidential appointments that mimic those of governing boards. Some governing boards, whatever their official license, operate more as referees among contending institutions than as educational policy leaders. Sometimes these relatively weak boards lack the formal authority that bolsters their ability to lead change. In other instances, powerful institutions, such as the state's land grant or research university, ally with legislative supporters to restrict the system's ability to make change.

> A few states have no statewide governing board or they have boards or agencies with minimal authority. New Jersey relies largely on the work of local campus governing boards, although those public university boards and their presidents voluntarily cooperate with the New Jersey Association of State Colleges and Universities.. Ohio eliminated its coordinating board in favor of a formidable state agency whose chief executive is a member of the governor's cabinet and an advisory board. Michigan's universities and their individual boards are famous for their defense of constitutionally guaranteed autonomy and the lack of other-than-voluntary statewide coordination.

Figure 7.1 Overview of State Systems

STRUCTURE	DESCRIPTION	STATES
Central administration	State higher education governing agency, complete with a central administration office that oversees all public two- and four-year institutions.	Alaska, Hawaii, Idaho, Kansas, Montana, Nevada, North Dakota, Rhode Island, South Dakota, Utah
Statewide or consolidated systems	Two consolidated governing systems for all public institutions exist, one that oversees the four-year colleges and universities, and the other, the two-year colleges.	Florida, Georgia, Iowa, Maine, Mississippi, New Hampshire, North Carolina, Oregon, Wisconsin, and Wyoming
Freestanding institutions	Four-Year institutions have their own independent governing boards (nine states). Two-year institutions are organized and administered separately. Some states may also have a state coordinating or governing agency.	Delaware, Kentucky, Michigan, New Jersey, New Mexico, Ohio, Virginia, Washington, West Virginia
Mixed structures of free standing institutions and systems	Combination of the above structures. Some have their own independent governing boards. Two-year institutions are organized and administered separately.	For example, Alabama, Arkansas, Colorado, Illinois, Indiana, Maryland, Missouri, Oklahoma, Pennsylvania, South Carolina, Vermont
Multiple large systems	Multiple large systems.	California, Louisiana, Minnesota, New York
State coordination	State higher education coordinating agency. The balance of power between institutions and coordinating boards shifts depending on the dynamics of regional politics, the governor's policy agenda, and the personalities of educational leaders.	For example, California, Colorado, Delaware, Kentucky, Louisiana, Minnesota, New Mexico, Ohio, Oklahoma, Virginia, Washington West Virginia

Source: Richard Novak, *An Overview of American Public Higher Education Governance* (AGB, 2009).

Great—and Changing—Expectations for System Boards

States' changing expectations for what systems should achieve have brought disappointment, conflict, and now renewed hope over the past 40 years. Allowing for variations among states, overlapping trends, and the dogged persistence of "old" missions even as contradictory new ones are set in place, there are three periods in the recent history of higher-education systems. The era of constraint during the late 1970s and early 1980s was succeeded in the 1990s by a loss of faith in the capacity of systems to manage higher-education. In this century, however, a keener awareness of the link between advanced education and economic prosperity has led policy makers to view systems and their boards as agents of change. Systems are now expected to apply their often-considerable authority to the tasks of getting more education to more people more quickly—and to do so at lower cost.

> *Only about one in five students completes a two-year college program after three years, and only about four in 10 completes a four-year degree within six years.*
> —JOHN IMMERWAHR and JEAN JOHNSON, "Squeeze Play 2010:
> Continued Public Anxiety on Cost, Harsher Judgments on How Colleges are Run"
> (Public Agenda and National Center for Public Policy and Higher Education, February 2010)

That Was Then...

In the 1960s and 1970s, the heyday of expansion of public colleges and universities, presidents and faculty members wanted to grow enrollments, campuses, facilities, and prestige so their institutions could advance to the next level in the academic hierarchy. Alarmed at rising costs and seemingly uncoordinated expansion, some policy makers dutifully called for more-rational allocation of public resources as powerful institutions and their advocates in state legislatures and the business community were espousing a philosophy of growth. One weary veteran of those conflicts observed accurately that in the face of growth pressures, systems were mere "'speed bumps' on the road to the inevitable."[11]

The chronic inability of systems to "just say no" to growth, or the trenchant criticism when they did, led to three consequences: Lightly bridled expansion of colleges and universities continued; many systems came to be seen as annoying, ineffectual, and irrelevant to the real challenges facing higher education and the nation; and states set about reducing their authority or eliminating them altogether. In a well-publicized 1993 critique, Patrick M. Callan, president of the National Center for Public Policy and Higher Education and a thoughtful critic of contemporary higher education's performance, raised several trenchant questions about the real costs of system bureaucracies and their threat to lay governance.[12]

---

[11] McGuinness, p. 209.

[12] Patrick M. Callan and Joni E. Finney, "By Design or Default?" (The California Higher Education Policy Center, 1993).

Almost as a fulfillment of Callan's critique, in the same year Governor Christine Todd Whitman of New Jersey eliminated that state's powerful coordinating board in favor of local campus boards. For a time, it looked as if systems in other states would decline in favor of a free-market model that allowed individual campuses and their boards to compete in the academic marketplace for students, resources, attention, and reputation.[13]

> *Systems can easily drift into a "middle muddling through" position in which they are neither providing policy and educational leadership on behalf of the state and broader society nor fostering diverse, well-managed campuses. Both roles are important. Compromising one at the expense of the other will not work.*
> –AIMS C. MCGUINNESS, "A Model for Successful Restructuring" in
> *Restructuring in Higher Education: What Works and What Doesn't* (Jossey-Bass, 1996)

... This Is Now

The tide has turned for state higher-education systems. Once derided as out-of-date bureaucracies no longer relevant in a dynamically competitive world, these powerful organizations are again heading toward a high-water mark in public expectations. States increasingly look to them to provide the foundations of economic opportunity and prosperity. Virtually every state with system governing or coordinating boards expects these boards to deliver on goals like the following:

- Increase educational effectiveness using measures such as retention-rate and graduation-rate improvement and higher achievement scores;

- Increase the quality and numbers of graduates in the STEM disciplines— science, technology, engineering, and mathematics—as well as other high-demand fields, especially health-related ones;

- Increase the flow through the educational pipeline from prekindergarten through the baccalaureate degree and beyond by aligning curricula and admissions standards more seamlessly with K–12 schools;

- Engage in applied research oriented toward commercialization, business development, and employment; and

- Improve operational efficiencies and reap scale economies by using the system's authority to control campus missions, program offerings, and collective-bargaining agreements and by centralizing legal, information management, technology purchasing, and other administrative functions.

In states like Wisconsin and North Carolina, system boards are hard at work exerting their already substantial authority to achieve state educational and economic priorities.

---

[13] Terrence MacTaggart, *Seeking Excellence through Independence: Liberating Colleges and Universities from Excessive Regulation* (Jossey-Bass, 1998).

Barriers to Statewide Change

Achieving the goals laid out in these mandates can be daunting. First, the traditions of shared governance give faculty and often staff members a larger voice in decisions than employees in almost any corporation or nonprofit enterprise. Yet serious change in the academy—especially if it requires adjusting the status quo in workload, degree requirements, curriculum, and other areas historically under faculty control— absolutely demands faculty engagement and endorsement. System boards tend to be more insulated from campus pressures than campus-based boards, and they can use this distance from academic centers of power to be more demanding about change.

Second, while the charge to system boards may be explicit, they share authority for making a difference with a host of state agencies and especially with legislators, who often display a vested interest in special treatment for their local colleges or universities and the constituents who work there as faculty or staff members. Board members in the University of Maine System met this reality head-on when they attempted to merge several smaller campuses in a good-faith response to public criticism of system costs. Shortly after the intent to merge became publicly known, powerful local representatives passed a new law, signed by the governor, denying the system this authority. Those close to that drama observed that the legislators feared the loss of jobs and prestige should the merger go through. In some cases, they wished to assert that at the end of the day, legislative will could always trump objectionable policy proposals from system boards. The lesson is that change requires boards that are adept at both making sound policy and managing the politics of change. What seem to be logical policy proposals need also to pass a political feasibility test if they are to survive in the public sector.

A third barrier is the fact that most systems must maintain equilibrium in the face of regional struggles around shifting political and economic strength. Sustaining political balance and managing competition among regions and institutions works against any change that seems to create winners and losers. Coping with the demands of ascendant regions for larger and more expensive institutions while accommodating the demands of stable or declining regions to sustain their institutions, often including high-cost research universities, is a dilemma nearly all system boards face. Board members frequently find themselves caught between loyalties to their geographic region and its institutions and their responsibility to serve the interests of the entire state. Simply coping with the wants and needs of such contending factions—and occasionally converting them into coalitions to pursue a common goal like a larger appropriation from the state (or these days, a lesser cut)—is the most that some systems can accomplish.

Coping vs. Leading

The demands for change in state higher-education systems are outstripping the pressures to sustain peace in the political valleys. Or, rather, citizens living in the valleys and the cities and suburbs alike are realizing that knowledge has become the essential economic resource and that states that educate more of their citizens to a higher level of competence are more likely to prosper. The board and executive leaders described in this chapter display the verve to corral parochial interests toward service of a statewide public agenda. Maryland's Effectiveness and Efficiency Initiative, the University of North Carolina Tomorrow program, and the Growth Agenda for Wisconsin reveal sustainable marriages of effective politics and good public policy.

There is a difference between system boards whose best efforts are to maintain the status quo and those that move the needle appreciably in educating students with the knowledge and skills needed to thrive in this globally competitive century (Figure 7.2).

Figure 7.2 Distinctions that Make a Difference in Changing State Systems

MAINTAINS STATUS QUO	BRINGS POSITIVE CHANGE
• Administration trumps leadership	• Leadership dominates administration
• Regulatory culture	• Change-oriented culture
• Academic preferences trump public needs	• State needs are top priority
• One-size-fits-all policies	• Recognizes institutional distinctiveness
• Caters to political interests	• Manages political interests
• Static budget allocations	• Resources follow strategy
• Little mission change	• Missions realigned with strategy

What are the levers of change that enable boards to make a difference in the educational achievement profile of their states? Some answers can be found in the experience of three highly effective systems—the University System of Maryland, the University of North Carolina System, and the University of Wisconsin System.

Economic Drivers of Change

After some discussion of alternative names for the University System of Maryland's change objective, the regents decided on a distinctly unpoetic but absolutely clear description: the Effectiveness and Efficiency Initiative. Their aim was to convince a skeptical legislature that Maryland's system could become measurably more efficient and cost effective. Goals for the initiative included preserving academic quality, enrolling more students, and increasing access for underserved populations. But all of these goals needed to be met at lower cost than business as usual would entail.

In describing the overarching theme of the University of North Carolina Tomorrow program, its architect, Erskine Bowles, the system president, declared the intent to move from a "supply-driven organization to a demand-driven one." Dismayed by the statistic that only one-third of North Carolina's college-age students were actually studying for a two- or four-year degree—less than half the number in Korea and well behind countries like Greece, Finland, Belgium, Ireland and Poland—the systemwide board of governors charged Bowles with initiating a campaign to bolster the state's economic competitiveness through higher education. A prominent goal of UNC Tomorrow was "improving the state's readiness to compete in global markets" by increasing access to higher education, especially among immigrant, minority and low-income groups; improving teacher education and measuring their effectiveness; and applying university research to economic development.

The relative prosperity of Wisconsin's neighbor to the west, Minnesota, provided one impetus and rationale for the Wisconsin regents' Growth Agenda for Wisconsin. In his many presentations to the legislature and across the Badger State, University of Wisconsin System President Kevin P. Reilly pointed out some compelling statistical comparisons. In 2008, 32 percent of Minnesota's adults held four-year degrees; the comparable number in Wisconsin was 26 percent, two points below the national average. As a consequence, according to Reilly, per capita income in Minnesota was $43,000, placing it 11th in the nation, while Wisconsin residents earned $5,000 less per capita and the state ranked 25th. The Growth Agenda for Wisconsin pursues such familiar goals as increasing access, applying university research to developing high-wage jobs, and improving operational cost effectiveness. But the most telling metric is the objective of increasing undergraduate degree production by 30 percent—from about 26,000 in 2009 to 33,700 by 2025.

Critical Success Factors in Systemwide Change

The boards of these three large systems adopted similar goals and change processes to better align the work of their universities with a "public agenda" for their states. All three set out to increase access, in part by focusing on previously underserved populations; to achieve measurable increases in degree production; to apply university-based research to economic and job growth; and to build stronger regional communities.

The University System of Maryland gave higher priority to cost effectiveness and produced some impressive results. The system achieved more than $200 million in cost savings; graduation rates improved beyond those of most public systems; tuition did not increase from 2005 to 2010; enrollment overall grew by 15,000 students without additional state support; and minority graduation rates rose to meet or surpass the most effective institutions in the country.

The North Carolina Board of Governors changed its criteria for approving new academic programs to ensure congruity with the goals of UNC Tomorrow. It added new standards to faculty promotion and tenure criteria, strongly encouraged campuses to revise general education, and changed the way it presented its budget request to the legislature—all to align with the economic priorities of UNC Tomorrow. Notable in North Carolina's plan is a data-based effort to reform teacher preparation that defines the quality of teacher-education programs in terms of measurably improved student performance in grades K–12.

Wisconsin's Board of Regents aligned its already strong accountability system to support the Growth Agenda. Regular quantitative reports on student preparation, graduation-rate increases, research funding, and other goals are presented and discussed at regents' meetings. The early returns on the Growth Agenda after three years are mostly positive: For example, UW System institutions are graduating more students overall and more in key STEM fields.

The Change "Campaign"

What do the three systems' change campaigns have in common? These systematic campaigns share several characteristics:

- Substantive policy goals that appeal to policy makers, opinion leaders, and the public;

- Sophisticated public and political communications programs to throw a positive light on the initiatives;

- Meaningful engagement of campus leaders, especially campus executives and faculty members;

- Recognition that campuses with differing missions would contribute to the statewide agenda in distinctive ways;

- Insistence on quantitative outcomes measures rather than anecdotes touting success; and

- Close working partnerships between the board and the executive in initiating the change and throughout the campaign.

We will now examine each of those characteristics in more depth.

Meaningful Policy Goals

All three campaigns worked toward similar policy goals that reflect a national public agenda. These goals explicitly address what is widely believed to be the formula for turning educational achievement into a strong competitive position for individuals and states. The goals depart from the traditional academic agenda, which favors exclusivity more than access, attributes low graduation rates more to academic rigor and student choice than institutional behavior, and, to use Erskine Bowles' terms, focuses more on production than on demand—that is, more on the values of academic preferences than public needs.

Emphasis on Public Communications and Relationships

Maryland's regents deliberately chose the name Effectiveness and Efficiency, often abbreviated as E&E, precisely because it communicated so well to legislators and the public the purpose of the change. The highly visible process in North Carolina included 11 well-publicized community listening forums attended by regents and the system president and provided opportunities for online and mail feedback. More than

10,000 North Carolinians had their voices heard. In Wisconsin, regent chairs joined President Kevin Reilly to barnstorm across the state touting the economic aspirations of the Growth Agenda. The intense public engagement in North Carolina reinforced already-strong legislative support. In Maryland and Wisconsin, the intentionally visible effort converted many skeptical legislators; in Wisconsin, base support increased by $21 million during a time of fiscal austerity.

Collaboration with Campus Presidents and Faculty Members

The chair of Maryland's regents, Clifford M.Kendall, and Chancellor William "Brit" E. Kirwan met often with faculty representatives. Clifford Kendall won over skeptics by asking, "Would you rather have an outside agency determine your future or the regents and the system that care about you?" In North Carolina, the chair of the statewide faculty assembly was a voting member of the UNC Tomorrow Commission. A Scholars Council made up of 14 distinguished professors from the UNC System researched trends and challenges, participated in the listening forums, and helped the staff draft the final report and recommendations. Faculty participation and support in all three state systems were especially important in light of the potential for controversy over putting economic goals ahead of traditional academic priorities. It should be noted, however, that the Maryland campaign's first objective was the preservation of academic quality, and sustaining quality remained a given in North Carolina and Wisconsin as well.

Campus presidents or chancellors played a major role in all three campaigns. They reported that their system boards took a personal interest in their perspectives and adjusted plans to recognize individual campus strengths. The top administrators helped shape the campaigns during regular meetings between campus and system leaders, participated in the community and campus listening sessions, and joined in persuading legislators that the reforms were credible.

Recognized Differences in Market Potential and Missions among Campuses

A standard and sometimes accurate criticism of system boards is that they endorse one-size-fits-all policies that ignore different campus missions and potential. The most adroit boards, like those in these three systems, build on these differences to yield better results and more cooperation. In Wisconsin, for example, regents found that the goals of the Growth Agenda could be achieved while allowing differential tuition at selected campuses. They approved higher tuition at the Eau Claire campus as long as the additional money was invested in high-impact practices designed to ensure higher graduation rates, a key Growth Agenda goal. Based on Brit Kirwan's recommendation, Maryland regents designated four institutions for high growth and for additional funding to support the increases in graduates. Rather than homogenize the campuses through one-size-fits-all policies, these system boards and their executives appear to have struck the right balance between campus individuality and the pursuit of collective public goals.

A Preference for Metrics over Anecdotes

Boards in all three systems insisted on comprehensive accountability systems and regular monitoring and updating. Wisconsin's UW Accountability Goals leave little room for doubt as to the relative success in achieving Growth Agenda goals. North Carolina's Board of Governors asked the universities to participate in a voluntary system of reporting results, and all agreed to do so. Maryland's system enabled the board to report accurately to the public and the legislature on substantial increases in faculty workload at both research and comprehensive universities. While heartwarming anecdotes extolling successful students and inspiring faculty members are an important part of communicating the value of higher education, a comprehensible set of metrics will go further in persuading a skeptical audience that the reform is genuine.

Integral Leadership

"We all arrived together" is how a Wisconsin regent characterized the conversational process that led the board and President Reilly to form the outline that became the Growth Agenda for Wisconsin. The board had sought out an executive highly familiar with Badger State culture and politics to build a closer relationship between the sprawling system and an often-disenchanted legislature. After eight years as either chancellor or vice chancellor of the statewide cooperative extension program, Kevin Reilly knew firsthand the likes and dislikes of the people and their representatives. He was the ideal choice for the relationship building that the regents had in mind. In North Carolina, Jim W. Phillips Jr., chair of the board of governors, also chaired the UNC Tomorrow Commission, and 10 board members served on the 28-member panel. Maryland's energetic board chair, Clifford Kendall, is widely credited with spearheading the E&E initiative and recognized for working closely with Brit Kirwan, who was president of the College Park campus for 10 years and then president of Ohio State University before returning to Maryland as chancellor. In all three cases, board chairs and board members played an active role in the conception, initiation, and delivery of the statewide campaigns led by their system executives.

Applying the Right Levers for Change
University System of Maryland • University of North Carolina • University of Wisconsin System

Most if not all of the nation's 60 or so systems nominally pursue a public-purpose agenda that includes the goals set forth in Maryland, North Carolina, and Wisconsin. But what accounts for the relative success of change in these three states—in addition to exceptionally talented and forceful board and executive leadership—is the methodical approach to change.

(For more on change at the University System of Maryland, University of North Carolina, and University of Wisconsin see Appendix.)

Lessons about Change at a Statewide Level

Accomplish the change agenda through a systematic campaign.
Substantive change is too complex and the barriers it must overcome too high for piecemeal efforts like pilot programs or purely voluntary cooperation to achieve much. A forceful, well-publicized campaign is essential. Give the campaign an appropriate name, vision statement, policy goals, public communications, metrics, and unified leadership. Employing expert panels of distinguished faculty members lends great credibility, especially if the panels issue well-researched reports.

Involve nonacademic stakeholders in the process.
Develop objectives that reflect the deepest hopes of the state's "ordinary-extraordinary" citizens for a better future. Feature higher education as a tool to position the state and its residents for competition in a global economy where knowledge and highly skilled workers tend to prosper. Involving external stakeholders may be especially important in state systems because of the political context and the need for community support. Including business and nonprofit leaders, policy makers, and opinion leaders will help convince the public that the change is not just driven by academics and higher-education administrators. Good ideas not imagined by the insiders who designed the campaign will inevitably emerge from these knowledgeable nonacademics.

Take advantage of the system's diverse institutional missions and strengths.
Do not expect all institutions to contribute equally when it comes to research. Recognize that they can contribute in different ways to increased graduation rates, depending on their location and student characteristics. But require all institutions to improve performance on the most-important objectives.

Tackle the challenging issues, such as teaching loads; program mergers, consolidations, and closures; and major reductions in personnel.
Bringing substantive change will require tough action on issues that are often considered the "third rails" of academic politics. Take advantage of the wide recognition that an environment of reduced resources is here to stay to restructure institutions and develop more sustainable business models.

Establish clear, measurable goals and systematically monitor progress against them.
Insist on concise metrics that enable the board to view improvements over past performance and make comparisons with other, high-performing systems. Monitor these measures regularly, offering praise when goals are met or exceeded, asking probing questions when they are not, and challenging leaders to do better.

***Maintain cohesion between campus and system executives and the board
on the importance and direction of the change campaign.***
The board must show visible support for campus leaders' efforts and work closely
with the system head on all phases of the campaign, from inception, to planning, to
participation in public sessions, to evaluation of results. In systems where there are no
campus boards, repeated examples of the system board's visible engagement sends a
powerful message about the board's dedication to change. Recognizing the opposition
to change that campus presidents often face, system boards should take every
opportunity to communicate their commitment to the change and show support
for campus leaders and their achievements.

Topics for Board and System Head Discussion

1. ***Regional and national context.*** How does our state compare with others in
   the region and the nation with respect to educational attainment and
   economic indicators? What do these data tell us about the policy goals we
   should pursue as a system?

2. ***Support for change.*** How does our system's governance culture—including
   the relationship between campuses and the system, the board's and system
   head's authority, and the respect for the board's role by the governor and
   legislature—support the board's ability to bring about change? What aspects
   of this culture need improvement to support board- and system-led change?

3. ***Goals and practices to emulate.*** What lessons from Maryland, North
   Carolina, and Wisconsin could be incorporated into our strategy? How
   would we need to adapt them to our circumstances?

Chapter 8

TAKING IT TO THE NEXT LEVEL: THE BOARD'S ROLE IN PURSUING HIGH ASPIRATIONS

A recurring theme in this book is the link between the board's fundamental responsibilities and its role in change. If the board's job is to safeguard the institution so that it can carry out its purpose for the benefit of students and society, it follows that sometimes the board must bring about substantive change. Crises, scandals, or catastrophes galvanize some boards to lead, guide, or otherwise contribute to change. Or, with less drama, early indicators of decline or a shift in the competitive environment may predict difficulties to come. Sometimes, however, the board of a pretty good college or university that is facing no particular threats simply wants to set higher aspirations, build a better institution, and achieve a more attractive, competitive position in the higher-education marketplace.

Consider these examples of board leadership that sparked movement to the logical next level of performance:

- ***Agnes Scott College***, a women's college in suburban Atlanta, enjoyed a robust endowment thanks to a substantial gift of Coca-Cola stock, but its appeal to capable students was declining due to a stale teaching and learning environment and uninspired marketing. Some faculty members speculated that despite the college's financial health, there might not be enough students to maintain its viability as a place to learn. Energetic board members took matters into their own hands, managed the graceful departure of a president, hired new leadership, reinvigorated fund raising, and worked actively with faculty members to revitalize the academic side. Agnes Scott became a sparkling example of excellence in higher education for women as it added signature buildings to its campus and achieved record enrollment.

- ***The University of Dubuque***, a seminary and college in the reformed Presbyterian tradition, faced a grim future, with declining enrollment, mounting debt, tired residence halls and academic and athletic facilities, as well as significantly impaired governance. The board hired a charismatic new president, a former seminary dean and pastor, who worked with it to fashion a fresh vision of becoming one of the best small Christian colleges. Dubuque has tripled enrollment, established a $71-million endowment, and rebuilt the campus to become the most attractive in the region.

- ***Trenton State College***, a middle-of-the road state institution in New Jersey's capital city, had few distinguishing qualities. A visionary board chair argued passionately that the state deserved a public university that offered a high-quality education to match the best private institutions in the state. Over

30 years, through three presidents, and amid state governance changes and declining state support, the college has advanced to the front ranks of public institutions. Renamed The College of New Jersey and located on a handsome campus with stunning Georgian architecture, TCNJ attracts and graduates in high numbers some of the best students in the region.

- Like many regional state universities, the **University of North Florida** in suburban Jacksonville was difficult to define. It lacked the research power of the University of Florida, the size and political heft of institutions in larger population centers, and the academic distinctiveness of the small, public, liberal arts New College in Sarasota, Fla. UNF assembled a remarkable team, including its intrepid board chair, a Naval Academy graduate and former submarine officer; a savvy and visionary president well versed in Jacksonville's issues and Florida politics; and its strong academic vice-president, a Haverford graduate. Today, UNF is well on its way to achieving recognition for service to its region at a national level of quality. It aims for the stature of outstanding medium-sized public universities like Miami University in Ohio.

There are many paths to the next level of excellence. In fact, determining the right destination is a crucial and difficult first step. These four institutions exerted a variety of board leadership roles to define new aspirations, cultivate the institution's distinctive strengths, and take steps to implement a vision of institutional quality.

This chapter addresses the following issues:

- What does it mean to reach for the next level of performance?
- What lessons can be learned from institutions that strive to become superior in their class?
- Why is board leadership essential to developing high-quality colleges and universities?
- What are the pitfalls to be avoided along the way?

How It Starts: What Motivates High Aspirations

Aspirations to move an institution to the next level of excellence can develop in two contexts: as the result of a crisis or in response to the insight that improved performance is possible. A crisis, either on the doorstep or forecast to appear, provides the springboard not just to fix immediate problems, but to strengthen the institution overall. Some boards and presidents seem to believe that dealing with the immediate peril constitutes the whole job, but these unfortunate souls are condemned to relive crises again and again. The most effective boards see problems as opportunities. A paradox of turnarounds is that the fall, or the near fall, inspires the best boards to raise expectations and find the right presidents to achieve them.

> *You can't develop a great institution without having a great board.*
> *The institution can't be any better than the board that governs it.*
> —SCOTT S. COWEN, President, Tulane University

Absent a crisis, high aspirations often stem from a board leader's belief that "we can do better." Chair Erna Hoover's vision in 1976 for a public college in New Jersey equal in quality to Princeton inspired changes that transformed Trenton State into The College of New Jersey. More recently, Chair Bruce Taylor from the University of North Florida, in partnership with President John Delaney, set in motion a deliberative process to take that regional university to a higher level of excellence. UNF faced no greater threats than other comprehensive public universities; it would have remained a well-regarded university had these leaders been content to preserve the status quo. But both the president and the board chair, and eventually the entire board, committed the university to a change process aimed at developing a regional university with national recognition for academic quality.

Whether spurred by an existential threat or simply motivated by confidence in potential, the boards and presidents featured in this chapter all embarked on journeys to bring their institutions to positions of stronger academic quality, greater financial strength, and enhanced attractiveness in the market for students, faculty members, and resources.

What Higher Aspirations Look Like

Colleges and universities that aspire to a higher level of excellence combine distinctive academic qualities and values with a sure instinct for what will work in the marketplace. In a board discussion at the University of Dubuque, the enrollment chief described this duality in terms of soft-drink marketing: "Think of the brand as the outside of the Coke can. We need a strong brand. But we also need to make sure the inside of the Coke can delivers the value our students and their families expect."

Superior institutions come in many shapes and sizes, well beyond the conventional hierarchy of the elites. Their boards accept and often embrace what George Keller calls the "ethos of capitalist competition"[14] while insisting on worthwhile educational aims. Virtually all measure themselves against the competition and their own past performance. A few represent the very best of their kind, but all offer substantial educational value for their students' investment of money, time, and hope. They are not elitist, but descriptors like "superior" and "uniquely excellent" are accurate enough. They strive to be superior in their league of competitors, but also to differentiate themselves from the competition.

---

[14] George Keller, *Transforming a College: The Story of a Little-known College's Strategic Climb to National Distinction* (The Johns Hopkins University Press), 2004 p. xi.

These institutions are on the move. They aspire to become better, more effective, and more widely respected because they believe in the value of what they offer, recognize the worth of a strong brand, and want their students to feel pride in graduating from a high-quality college or university. It is hard to imagine a board member or president who would not share these aspirations. But there is an immense difference between those who espouse lofty goals and those who take the actions necessary to actually achieve them. Boards and presidents with the second mindset want to build institutions that:

- Aspire to excel in ways that capture the genius of the place and inspire their institutional communities;
- Outperform their competitors and similar institutions based on meaningful, measurable educational outcomes;
- Develop distinctive features that represent value to students, donors, and the public; and
- Foster a brand or reputation that links their genuine internal strengths with appetite in the marketplace.

Practical Advantages to Aiming High

Setting a future course for the whole institution with waypoints for its passage offers several psychological and practical advantages. This holistic approach:

- Provides a fresh vision that builds on inherent strengths and inspires the campus community to put forth its best efforts;
- Defines a clear aspiration coupled with a plan that includes criteria for choosing among options, especially when deciding where and where not to put money;
- Gives the institution a competitive edge in marketing to potential students;
- Contributes to the diversity of students' educational options; and
- Energizes fund raising, helps define case-statement goals, and gives donors more-compelling reasons to be generous.

Institutional Trajectories: Ideal and Actual

Figure 8.1 illustrates both an idealized upward trajectory, the kind that appears in lectures but never in reality, along with a hypothetical curve depicting the pitfalls, reversals, and surprises that slow or interrupt movement upward in real life. While a recession, unfortunate work interruption, or new competition—a career-focused proprietary institution for example or a community college offering four-year degrees at bargain-rate tuition—may impede progress for a time, occasional windfalls will help move things along more quickly. The point is that leaders seeking to raise their institutions to a higher level need to fortify their spirits and those of their coworkers for the inevitable nasty surprises, be prepared to move quickly to seize the opportunity that good fortune brings, and through it all persevere.

Figure 8.1 Institutional Trajectories: Idealized and Actual

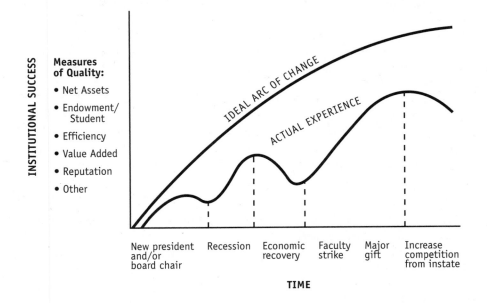

Lessons from Aspiring Boards

What distinguishes a board that enjoys some success in the pursuit of excellence and competitiveness? Other chapters highlight general features of change-adept boards, such as enlightened awareness of the board's appropriate role in bringing about change (Chapter 2), a productive working relationship between the board and president (Chapter 3), and intentional recruitment of change-minded trustees (Chapter 6). But in addition to having those attributes, boards that lead their institutions to a new threshold of quality share five habits of leadership that offer lessons for other boards to reflect upon and apply to their own situations:

1. Setting the right aspirations;

2. Reaching convergence around aspirational goals;

3. Developing a strategic plan linked to the budget and quantified milestones;

4. Understanding and pursuing academic quality; and

5. Marketing and branding the institution's distinctiveness.

Setting the Right Aspirations

Each change-oriented board described in this chapter—and most of the boards featured in this book—aspires to higher levels of excellence in its own performance and in that of the institution it governs. But targeting the right goals requires much deliberation and some intuition as well. The board at Agnes Scott, for example, could have shifted to a coeducational strategy, as many of its peers have done, in order to build a larger student cadre. But this would have meant a radical change in the true genius of the college: providing an exceptional educational opportunity for women only. Through innovations such as the Atlanta Semester, which prepares women for civic-leadership roles, the student-run honor system, and a global experience, Agnes Scott has achieved its goal of becoming, in Loren Pope's words, "one of the best colleges around." [15]

Questions for Board Members

- Is the aspiration clear enough to be widely and quickly understood?
- Is it bold enough to inspire yet realistic enough to be achieved?
- Does it build on institutional strengths and values in a fresh way?
- Does it enjoy reasonably broad support within and outside the campus?
- Will it help advance our institution and better serve the needs of students and society?
- If it is a long-term aspiration, are worthwhile intermediate steps identified?
- How will the board amass the resources to pursue this goal?

Reaching Convergence around Aspirational Goals

For this discussion, attention is concentrated in two realms: the board's work and the administration's work. First, the board's work—its conversations with the president, the policies it puts in place, the metrics it reviews, and so on—must align with the institution's strategic intentions. For example, a board that endorses the strategy of becoming one of the best colleges of its type, but gives this goal short shrift in its budget deliberations, fund raising, and academic and student-service committee work, is not doing enough to sustain the new trajectory. The second area of convergence falls more squarely within the administration's responsibility and includes significant institutional actions and policies, such as preparing case statements for capital campaigns, accreditation self-studies, reports and publications, budget allocations, and criteria for hiring, retaining, and promoting faculty members.

---

[15] Loren Pope, *Colleges that Change Lives: 40 Schools that Will Change the Way You Think About Colleges,* 2nd ed. (Penguin, 2006), p. 107.

The University of North Florida illustrates both types of convergence in pursuit of its strategic goal of achieving national recognition for quality (Figure 8.2). The board revised its meeting format to include more time devoted to strategy, greater opportunity for upstream discussions, regular in-depth conversations with the president over options and challenges, more frequent interactions with students and faculty members, and reviews of the institution's well-developed metrics for evaluating the preparedness of incoming students, graduation rates, and other performance variables. While the work of each action surrounding the core goal is the responsibility of administrators and faculty members, the board has studied all of them and participates actively in several, including leadership in the comprehensive campaign; selection of flagship programs and decisions about their funding; discussions of the interplay among measures of success, such as admissions standards and persistence rates; and their evaluation of their own development as a board.

Figure 8.2 Convergence: Components of Change

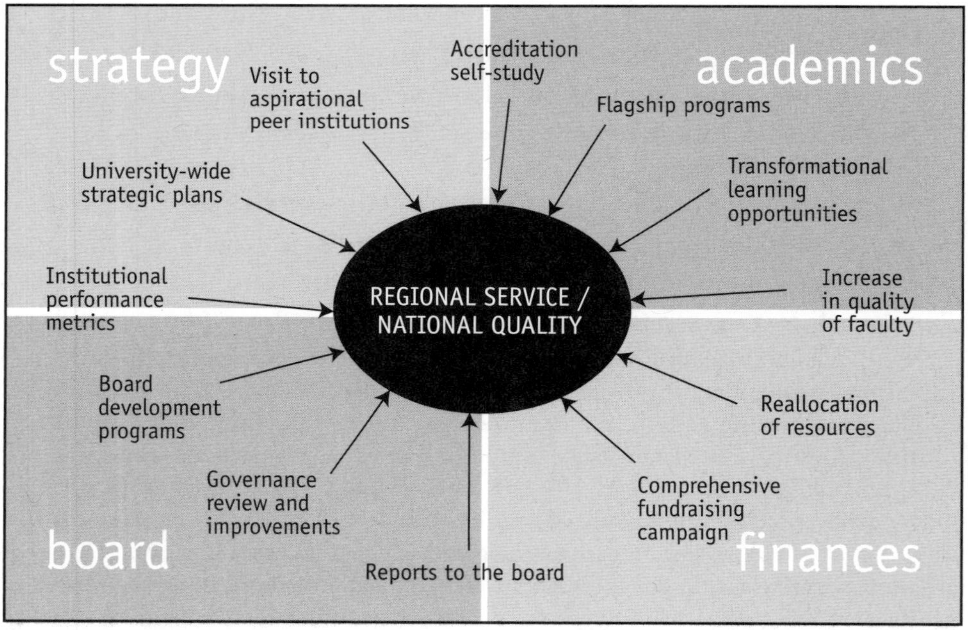

By insisting on evidence of in-depth convergence around the core aspiration, boards can help overcome the fragmentation that is inherent in the decentralized academy. They can exercise appropriate oversight without micromanaging if they are attentive to the alignment of significant institutional actions and policies with core aspirations for improvement.

Questions for Board Members

- Are we well informed about institutional actions and policies and confident that they match our aspirations for improvement?
- Does the board's regular work, including board meetings, focus on our core aspirations?
- Does the development committee's work reflect educational priorities?
- Does the board engage in questioning and dialogue about the key areas of convergence?

Developing a Strategic Plan Linked to the Budget and Quantified Milestones

The boards of the institutions profiled in this chapter helped develop practical plans for achieving their aspirations and then endorsed those plans. Hardheaded financial strategizing joined to the plan is especially crucial in recessionary times. Many of the private colleges constructed sophisticated budget tools to project revenues and expenses three to five years into the future. Because of their dependence on state support, the public institutions developed alternative planning scenarios. All of these plans are working documents, regularly discussed by the board and revised to reflect goals achieved, new opportunities, and the occasional instance where an initiative just did not work.

Questions for Board Members

- Are our plans realistic and completely grounded in fiscal realities?
- Are metrics comparing current and past performance included?
- Is the plan tied to the president's evaluation and compensation?
- Is the plan central to our discussions at board meetings?
- Is the plan central to our evaluations of our own performance?

Understanding and Pursuing Academic Quality

Institutions that aspire to a higher level of excellence understand what academic quality is and set high standards for achieving it. They pursue learning effectiveness, measured in terms of what students know and can do, and program effectiveness, measured in terms of faculty and staff performance. They appreciate hearing anecdotes depicting successful students and star faculty members, but they insist on evidence of learning gains as well. For example, University of Dubuque board members regularly debate what "best" means as they aspire to become one of the best small Christian universities. From one perspective, the institution should exploit its brand awareness to attract a better-prepared student body and increase its prestige, as defined in conventional terms. From another perspective, "best" means being most effective in enabling its largely first-generation students from diverse ethnic and geographic backgrounds to succeed. In a strategy that the board endorsed after robust conversation, Dubuque is advancing on both fronts.

Questions for Board Members

- Have we discussed how our distinctive academic programs work to enhance the institution's reputation for quality?
- Do we use appropriate metrics that reveal deep evidence of quality and success?
- Do we compare features like student retention, graduation rates, and engagement in campus life with metrics from similar institutions?
- Do we give the same attention to academic affairs as to budget, finance, and fund raising in our committee work and board meetings?

Marketing and Branding the Institution's Distinctiveness

Aspiring colleges and universities market and brand their distinctiveness. Signature programs like the Lester Wendt and Michael Lester Wendt Character Initiative at the University of Dubuque shape the students' educational experience and act as a powerful inducement to attend. This program provides scholarship support to selected students who are interested in the meaning of character development, infuses discussion on issues of character in every aspect of campus life, and challenges faculty members to enrich their teaching with discussions of character development. This asset, like the Odyssey program at Hendrix College described in Chapter 4, is a signature educational feature that figures prominently in marketing the university to students and families who seek a values component in their college choice.

Questions for Board Members

- Is the board versed in concepts and practices of higher-education marketing and reputation building?
- Do we discuss how our distinctive qualitative features contribute to a worthwhile educational experience and serve as effective marketing tools?
- Do we interact with the institution's enrollment-management professionals and understand their strategies as well as the competitive realities they face?
- Do we understand why some applicants choose other institutions and why others drop out or transfer?
- Do we take steps to ensure that we deliver on the promises that our recruiters make to students?

The good news is that other schools are copying Odyssey, but this imitation is the bad news too. Next year, our objective is to develop what the campus calls Odyssey 2.0.

—J. TIMOTHY CLOYD, President, Hendrix College

Why Board Leadership Is Essential

Achieving high aspirations is nearly impossible without active board leadership. Individual board members can provide the critical spark that puts an institution on a positive upward course. In a frequently repeated pattern, board leaders recognized that the status quo was not acceptable, convinced fellow board members that change was needed, worked with the current president and eventually recruited a new one, and partnered with that new executive to plan a better future.

In addition to taking action at a crucial moment in an institution's history, board members perform at least four other vital tasks in enabling transformation. They act as custodians of the brand; build a constructive partnership between the board and the president; ensure continuity between presidents; and provide generous personal support.

Custodians of the Brand

Vigilant protection of the institution's reputation in the midst of change is a special calling. Desperate times may demand desperate measures, but those choices still must be well calculated to advance the cause and not damage it. Board members can serve as a check on dubious new partnerships or programs that promise short-term relief but risk longer-term harm. Contracting with questionable recruiters in the United States or abroad to build enrollment, offering continuing education through agencies not fully under the institution's control, and similar schemes require an alert board that is willing to scrutinize and say "no" to suspicious associates and their ideas. The decision not to pursue a relationship with a particular for-profit enterprise at the University of Dubuque illustrates this custodial function.

Constructive Partnership between Board and President

The partnership between the board and the president is the essential relationship for positive change. In addition to promoting trust, amicability, and candor, the board must respectfully challenge the president to rethink strategies, reevaluate senior staff, and consider doing still more to reach aspirations. In return, board members should be open to challenges from their president when, for example, he or she asks if board members can do more or questions the goals they set. Bright, experienced people engaging in unfettered dialog almost always beget better ideas than either party might have developed in isolation. This spirit of openness to intelligent and usually enjoyable debate characterized all the board meetings we witnessed.

Continuity between Presidents

The board as an entity, separate from its individual members, exists as long as the institution does and far beyond the tenure of any single president. The board is a reassuring presence during presidential transitions. But even more important, the most-effective boards shape a new presidency beginning with the hiring process and the charge to the new executive. At a minimum, alert boards structure a presidency through the problems and challenges they articulate to candidates. When the board has endorsed a still-viable strategic plan, for example, seeking a president who can carry the plan forward is necessary board work. Changing strategic direction with each leadership change is inconsistent with long-term improvement. Attentive board members who are actively engaged in visioning, planning, and monitoring progress can ensure continuity and growth.

The three presidents who continued the advance of The College of New Jersey from an institution with mean SAT scores of 890 to mean scores of 1243 and from very generous admissions to 10,150 applications for 1,375 spots illustrate the importance of continuity along a strategic path. Clayton Bower (1971–1980) supported Erna Hoover's vision of a high-quality institution and pursued a "smaller but better" agenda. Harold Eickhoff (1980–1999) focused on the Georgian Colonial style of the campus, secured the name change, and with powerful board support helped establish a full-fledged, autonomous, college governing board after the demise of the state's coordinating board. Barbara Gitenstein (1999-present) focuses on attracting ever-more-able students and, working with faculty members, she has strengthened the curriculum. Adrian Tinsley, herself a former college president at Bridgewater State College and a student of the change at TCNJ, writes that "the board of trustees should receive considerable credit for that consistency of vision … and singleness of purpose" that led them to select three able presidents who continued the college 's upward trajectory. [16]

Generous Personal Support

Board members who make the institution the top priority in their philanthropy, who have the means to contribute transformational gifts, and who align their giving with the most important institutional directions are essential to building top-quality colleges and universities. Even in public institutions, where the expectations for giving may be different and individuals' wealth may be less, board members can be persuasive advocates to policy makers and grant-making agencies. Virtually every board member at the institutions profiled in this chapter contributes both financially and through their time, talent, and contacts. The University of North Florida is notable for board member support of its strong academic flagship programs, which are designed to address regional needs at a national level of excellence. Thus, trustee Luther Coggin underwrote the well-regarded college of business, which bears his name, and Chair Bruce Taylor supported the university's Coastal Biology Program, a critical area for the northeast portion of an isthmus state.

---

[16] Adrian Tinsley, "Academic Revitalization: Fulfilling the Turnaround Promise," in Terrence MacTaggart, ed., *Academic Turnarounds: Restoring Vitality to Challenged American Colleges and Universities* (ACE and Greenwood, 2007), p. 50.

Dare to Imagine a Better Future

The greatest impediment to moving to a higher level of quality is the unwillingness to imagine that a much stronger and more vital institution is possible. What might be thought of as objective impediments—for example, being located in a sparsely populated or unattractive area or lacking endowment or wealthy sponsors—are actually less daunting than attitudinal barriers and mental mistakes. Among the most common barriers are murky or unrealistic aspirations; the inability to deliver on the promise of a high-quality educational experience; a focus on solving problems instead of building the institution; and an identity defined in terms of national rankings.

Murky or Unrealistic Expectations

Aspirations are unlikely to be achieved if they are unclear, open to differing interpretations, difficult to measure, or hopelessly unrealistic. Taken to the extreme, unachievable goals can not only mislead the university community, but also potentially destroy it. Institutions that seek premier status as the university of choice in a region or a field still need to define what those terms mean in practical, quantified ways. Part of the success story of The College of New Jersey involves the trenchant clarity of goals set by the board and several presidents, as well as their discipline in pursuing them. While the college offers a few master's degree programs, the president and the board are adamant that a high-quality undergraduate education is the priority.

Promise vs. Reality

If the brand represents an institution's general reputation in the minds of the public, including students and those who influence them, then the brand promise is the assurance that the college or university will deliver what it claims to offer. The link between promise and reality is not an item for boards to accept on faith alone. The board should be alert to the evidence that their institution's assertion of its commitment to student success, for example, is reflected in its resource allocations, its academic strategies to help students succeed, and its graduation rates and measures of success after graduation. The board's promise to the public, not to mention accrediting agencies, is that the institution delivers to students what its promotional literature claims. As a practical matter—in this world of high-speed communications and widely available metrics comparing an institution with its competitors—failure to keep the promise means that failure in the market for enrollment and support will soon follow.

Problem Solving in Isolation

A board's initial response to a crisis takes the form of emergency action to keep the enterprise afloat. This problem-centric approach enables leaders to concentrate on one challenge at a time: changing the institution's cost structure, developing more-attractive programs, hiring more able staff, or engaging in more-aggressive fund raising. But before long, to avoid the pattern of lurching from crisis to crisis, many boards and presidents seeking positive change should begin to address the underlying flaws that left the institution vulnerable in the first place.

The weakness in the problem-centric approach lies in its fragmentation. Fixing problem areas more or less in isolation does represent positive change, but it does not result in a substantially stronger and more competitive institution. Plugging the hole in a leaky boat will keep it afloat, but a patch alone will not take it far or fast toward the horizon.

The Tyranny of the Rankings

Despite evidence that the ubiquitous "best colleges" rankings from *U.S. News & World Report* actually have only modest influence on college choice, the existence of rankings of all sorts reflects the human passion for simplifying distinctions through hierarchy. While it is a mistake to ignore the rankings, it is a more serious error to define an institution's identity in terms of this constantly moving target.

While academics criticize the simplification that comes with the parade of top 50 this or second-tier that, college Web sites highlight any reasonably high placements the institution can find. With the ever-expanding array of rankings, of course, there is scarcely an institution that doesn't get high marks from somebody for something. In light of this maelstrom of indicators, the best course of action for aspiring institutions, in the words of a Widener University board member, is to "run your own race." Selecting indicators that align with institutional goals—which indeed are likely to include some from *U.S. News* and other sources—provides a surer sign of institutional progress or its lack than the vagaries of the changing criteria and categories of the ranking industry.

A Steady Upward Trajectory

Although some boards seem reluctant to accept the need for turning around their beleaguered institutions, other boards have realized that change requires their active intervention to break a pattern of performance that was ordinary at best and lackluster at worst. While Agnes Scott had one of the nation's highest endowments per student, it faced dwindling enrollment and an increasingly unattractive position in the marketplace for the best students seeking a women's college. The board, inspired by the leadership of its chair, Joseph R. Gladden, worked actively with faculty to right-size the academic program to reflect actual student enrollment, revised endowment spending to fuel investments in more-attractive programs and facilities, and reinvigorated the college's culture to achieve true excellence in programs and student services.

Lacking an impressive endowment, the University of Dubuque fell on especially hard times in the mid-1990s. Enrollment and revenues dropped at this chronically tuition-dependent institution; the campus appeared fatigued and uninspiring; and board-faculty relationships were highly dysfunctional, with a large segment of the faculty apparently believing that it was the real governing entity. Dubuque's board refused to enter into a partnership with a for-profit enterprise that may have ensured survival because it would have been at the cost of damage to Dubuque's mission and reputation. That commitment underpinned one of the most remarkable turnarounds in institutional fortunes on the American higher-education scene.

As publicly supported institutions, The College of New Jersey and the University of North Florida were not likely to go out of business, but without exceptional board intervention, they were not destined to become great institutions either. The story of TCNJ Chair Erna Hoover, who insisted that the people of New Jersey deserved a public college equal in quality to the finest private schools in the state, has been chronicled elsewhere in this book. The turn from an ordinary state college to one with acceptance rates, incoming student test scores, and graduation figures that rival some of the best institutions in the country simply would not have occurred without the commitment to excellence that Hoover and subsequent board leaders showed over some 30 years. Equally as important is the consistency of vision; the college's transformation has become integral to the institution's success.

The words crystallizing the vision of the University of North Florida to become a "regional university of nationally recognized excellence" came from provost Mark Workman, but the concept grew from the aspirations of the long-serving board chair, Bruce Taylor, and the school's remarkable president, John Delaney. While UNF is in the early stages of its journey from a very good state university to a great one, its board and president are taking the right steps to become one of the best comprehensive public institutions in the country.

Boards that Galvanized Change

In most of these institutions, a leadership vacuum meant that no one but the board was positioned to initiate the necessary change. After the faculty at Agnes Scott gave the president a vote of no confidence, the board arranged a respectful departure while maintaining public support. With no permanent executive at the helm, the board stepped in to adjust programs, establish a working relationship with the faculty, and recalibrate the college's orientation toward enrollment growth and high brand value before hiring a new president to continue this upward trajectory.

Dubuque's board chair served as interim president for two years before a new president was hired to sustain the institution's traditional Christian mission while increasing enrollment, building endowment, and revitalizing the campus. Through three long-serving presidents, the board of The College of New Jersey has championed the mission of public institutional excellence. It has ensured that each new executive addresses the challenges of the day, usually financial, that threaten the persistence of Erna Hoover's dream. The University of North Florida is the exception to this pattern of board intervention during a leadership hiatus, as both the board chair and the president, simultaneously and in partnership, galvanized attention to seek higher levels of excellence within the public university framework.

Boards and Presidents as Partners in Change Leadership

While boards may galvanize and initiate change, they need a president, usually a new president, to carry out the new agenda over time. Agnes Scott retained an entrepreneurial alumna, Mary Brown Bullock, to carry out the redirection established by the board. By the time she retired in 2006, the institution had exceeded the enrollment goal of 1,000 students, rebuilt the campus, and largely restored its brand reputation as one of the south's exceptional colleges for women. During this period, the board remained active. It revised the endowment spending policies to, as one board member put it, "invest in the college, not the stock market"; achieved a more collegial relationship with the faculty; and lent its expertise to marketing the college.

The University of Dubuque had the good fortune to hire former seminary dean and Presbyterian pastor Jeffrey F. Bullock as its president. Bullock (who is not related to Mary Brown Bullock) led the way in tripling enrollment to nearly 2,000, quadrupling endowment to $71 million, and converting a tired campus into a showpiece for student learning and living. The board remains active both in helping to shape the vision of the university and in providing generous support, including for a stellar new athletics and health facility, University Science Center, and new student housing.

The College of New Jersey's board has displayed a remarkable level of consistency in selecting and supporting presidents who share its singleness of purpose in sustaining one of the nation's top public colleges. The board of the University of North Florida remains an energetic partner with the president—with generous donations by any standard, much less that of a public institution, regular discussions of how becoming a nationally recognized comprehensive university affects student access, and close attention to its own decision-making processes.

Aspiring Boards, High-Caliber Institutions
Agnes Scott College • The College of New Jersey • University of Dubuque • University of North Florida

As diverse as these four institutions are in mission, size, and governance, together they illustrate three recurring themes in the narratives of boards that lead their institutions to higher levels of performance and reputation. Agnes Scott and the University of Dubuque are private institutions in the Presbyterian tradition. TCNJ enjoys its own governing board; so does UNF, but it also operates within the Florida public university system, which has its own statewide governing board. In spite of these differences, all of these institutions offer lessons to boards seeking to be effective in turning around troubled or underperforming schools. These institutions share:

- A turnaround trajectory that moved them from ordinary performance at best to something better than any earlier high point;
- The reality that board leadership provided the essential leverage, without which the change might never have occurred; and
- The hiring of exceptionally able presidents to move them forward in collaboration with the board, with the locus of change leadership shifting to the new executive over time.

(For more on change at Agnes Scott College, The College of New Jersey, University of Dubuque, and University of North Florida see Appendix.)

Lessons about Striving for the Next Level

Recognize that at times only the board can intervene to start a turnaround.

When there is no one else to supply a fresh vision for a college or university, or its financial condition is deteriorating and the current executive seems unable to staunch the flow, it remains for the board, inevitably under the leadership of a strong chair, to intervene in the institution's affairs to set a new direction. Agnes Scott probably would not have reemerged from a period of decline without the board chair's active intervention following a faculty expression of lack of confidence in the president. A board chair set Trenton State College on the path to becoming the exceptional public college it is today. The board at the University of Dubuque committed itself to its historic mission and to finding a new president to revitalize the institution. The chair and president resolved together to move the University of North Florida to a higher level of excellence.

Whether acting with little or no support from a beleaguered or management-oriented president or operating in close partnership with an able executive, sometimes there is no substitute for board intercession in the affairs of a college or university to set it on a better path.

In bringing change, maintain clarity of mission and vision.

After serious debate, all four institutions pursued strategies of strengthening their historic missions rather than abandoning them. Agnes Scott's board chose not to follow the pattern of many peer women's colleges that have begun accepting men. The board determined to become preeminent again as a college for women. Trustees at Dubuque also faced a fork in the road and took the avenue they felt was most consistent with their reformed Presbyterian tradition. While TCNJ gradually developed higher admissions standards and now attracts many more applicants than it can accept, it remains true to its progressive mission of providing a superior education at public-college tuition rates. And UNF finds itself squarely in the mainstream of public institutional missions by giving equal emphasis to regional service and national excellence.

Ensure a three-part alignment among strategic aspirations, the work of the board, and institutional budgets and other major activities.

Surprisingly often there are gaps between what the board and president say they aspire to achieve, how the board actually spends its time, and budget allocations and other major college or university activities. Saying does not make it so, but systematic action might. Mapping graphically the link between aspirations, board agendas, committee tasks, and policy decisions, along with the flow of dollars and the goals of major initiatives like marketing efforts, campaign case statements, and accreditation studies is a good way to check on this essential feature of actually achieving change.

Aim high.

Failure to move a college or university to the next level of excellence begins with a failure of imagination. The unspoken belief that the institution can probably survive but not become much better is a recipe for mediocrity. The University of North Florida may well become nationally recognized for the quality of its academic programs in northeast Florida, but it will do so only because its leaders imagined a brighter future. To be sure, a vision of unique excellence is a necessary, but not the sole, requirement for greatness. The more mundane work of planning, communicating, allocating resources, and setting policies that demand better performance must be directed toward a high but achievable vision.

Topics for Board and President Discussion

1. ***Positive aspirations.*** Have we set clear, realistic, and engaging aspirations that will advance the quality and reputation of our institution?

2. ***Board engagement.*** Do the board chair and the president work together to support each other, keep the board informed, and encourage active questioning and dialogue about our aspirations during board meetings?

3. ***Strategic plan.*** Does the strategic plan include realistic projections and measurable outcomes in service of the fresh vision or new goals for our institution? Do we use the plan to stimulate discussion about our aspirations?

4. ***Board evaluation.*** Do we assess our performance, with the assistance of an objective outsider or a devoted board committee, in terms of our goal of substantially improving the institution we govern as well as the standards of good governance practice?

5. ***Presidential evaluation.*** Do we evaluate our president, and ask him to assess his own performance, against goals we have set for the institution as well as criteria for effective practice in presidential leadership?

EPILOGUE

Change for the Better

The future is not a result of choices among alternative paths offered by the present, but a place that is created—created first in mind and will, created next in activity. The future is not some place we are going to, but one we are creating. The paths to it are not found but made, and the activity of making them changes both the maker and the destination.

—JOHN H. SCHAAR, Professor Emeritus, University of California, Santa Cruz

If more boards and presidents framed their perspectives on change using this inspirational notion of the future, change might be less threatening, and building a stronger, better, healthier college or university might be easier and infinitely more rewarding. In truth, many change-adept boards and presidents are already creating brighter futures for their institutions. No matter what the impetus may be, they view the prospect of change in a positive light and the process of change as a journey of institutional growth and improvement.

Lessons Learned from Change at Academic Institutions

Being a high-performing board means being a change-adept board, a board that helps its college, university, or system change for the better. Board members, in collaboration with their presidents, can no longer passively hold their institutions in trust. They must actively govern. To do so, as evidenced in the lessons learned from the 18 institutions we studied, requires a deep and shared understanding of three integrated areas of leadership:

1. ***Change:*** Change often encounters resistance at the institutional and the individual level. The board may be in the best, and sometimes only, position to initiate a change process. That process, however, must include collaboration with the president, faculty members, and other key constituents. Often times, the change process must be led and managed as an institution-wide campaign.

Lessons Learned about Change

(The chapters that focus on each specific lesson are mentioned in parenthesis.)

- Prepare for the reality that not all board members will buy into the change. (Chapter 2)
- Appreciate the kind and depth of change required. (Chapter 2)
- Recognize the trenchant aversion to change that often exists in the academy. (Chapter 2)
- Recognize the occasions when the board must step forward to initiate change. (Chapter 3)

- Be prepared to work closely with the faculty during the change process. (Chapter 3)
- Match board action to the stages of change. (Chapter 4)
- Recognize that the presidency will always be a work in progress. (Chapter 5)
- Accomplish the change agenda through a systematic campaign. (Chapter 7)
- Involve nonacademic stakeholders in the change process. (Chapter 7)
- Maintain cohesion between campus and system executives and the board on the importance and direction of the change campaign. (Chapter 7)
- Recognize that at times only the board can intervene to start a turnaround. (Chapter 8)

2. **Strategy and Metrics:** Change often begins with a reconsideration of the mission, involves an inclusive process of visioning, and requires clarity of both. Successful strategies build on institutional strengths and core competencies, but they also require tackling thorny problems and difficult dilemmas. Strategies should push the institution with ambitious aspirations. They need to be converted into metrics so that leaders have clear, measurable goals against which to monitor progress. Then, the cycle begins anew, as strategy is never done.

Lessons Learned about Strategy and Metrics
- Refreshing the vision is a joint effort. (Chapter 3)
- Set clear, quantifiable strategic objectives. (Chapter 5)
- Take advantage of the system's diverse institutional missions and strengths. (Chapter 7)
- Tackle the challenging issues such as teaching loads; program mergers, consolidations, and closures; and major reductions in personnel. (Chapter 7)
- Establish clear, measurable goals and systematically monitor progress against them. (Chapter 7)
- In bringing change, maintain clarity of mission and vision. (Chapter 8)
- Aim high. (Chapter 8)

3. **Good Governance:** Change in academic institutions relies on good governance. Leadership starts with having the right people in the right places—on the board and in the president's office. Because change is often turbulent, it requires strong commitment, flexible leadership, and tenacious teamwork. Equipped with a realistic sense of its own performance, the board needs to respect the balance of power and interests at play in a college, university, or system. Board members should carefully calibrate their focus and efforts to the institution's shifting needs.

Lessons Learned about Good Governance

- Change requires strong partnership between the board and the president. (Chapter 2)
- Bring the right people with the right expertise on board. (Chapter 4)
- Generate exceptional personal commitment from board members. (Chapter 4)
- Make teamwork part of board culture. (Chapter 4)
- Make board service feel compelling. (Chapter 4)
- Build appreciation for the equilibrium of governance. (Chapter 4)
- Use committees and board expertise appropriately to vet strategic issues and advance strategic initiatives. (Chapter 5)
- Be intentional and strategic about board composition and board development. (Chapter 5)
- Focus the nominating process on alignment with the institution's strategic direction, not personal relationships with the president or board members. (Chapter 6)
- Set specific criteria, including openness to positive change, in the process of recruiting new board members. (Chapter 6)
- Diversifying a board with new members requires diplomacy and compassion when it comes to saying goodbye to long-serving board members. (Chapter 6)
- Look to advisory committees and similar groups as fertile ground for recruiting new board members. (Chapter 6)
- Self-assessment is a prerequisite to building a more change-adept board. (Chapter 6)
- Ensure a three-part alignment between strategic aspirations, the work of the board, and institutional budgets and other major activities. (Chapter 8)

Practices of Change-Adept Boards

What separates such boards from those that grapple less successfully with change? Based on the characteristics of boards described in this book, certain principles emerge. They seem to capture the underlying attitudes and practices of boards that have an astute understanding of the nature of change and the essential change-leadership qualities for a college or university setting. While no set of "habits" or "success factors" will constitute the last word on governance effectiveness, most high-functioning, change-adept boards exhibit seven qualities:

1. They seize opportunities to create positive change.
2. They adopt high aspirations for the institution, the president, and the board.
3. They align the work of the board with the institution's top priorities and change agenda.

4. They attract, support, and reward able presidents, who are prepared to lead change, while observing their performance over time.

5. They respect the equilibrium of governance by honoring board responsibilities and boundaries, even as they remain deeply engaged in guiding change.

6. They evaluate and reflect on individual and collective performance, as well as support for change, and then they make the right choices.

7. They attract and develop each board member with an eye toward his or her potential for change leadership, and deepen his or her personal commitment to the institution and its values.

Not surprisingly, those are also the positive habits of high-performing boards generally, although here we emphasize the board's change-leadership role.

1. Seize opportunities to create positive change.

"What are your goals for your term as chair?" a student reporter asked an incoming board chair. "Before I answer your question," the chair replied, "I'll have to confirm what our university and our board need." Although this chair had a good sense of what lay ahead, he was focused on the university rather than on a personal agenda. Scandals and crises, though by definition unanticipated, regularly thrust the opportunity to take positive action into the hands of the board. Other situations demanding board leadership are less dramatic but no less significant. Being attentive to simmering problems before they become crises enables astute boards to act in a timely way to strengthen the institution, the board, and often both.

When American University experienced a scandal precipitated by excessive presidential compensation and spending, the board looked beyond the immediate issue to focus on its own performance. Board members accepted responsibility for governance lapses, instituted sweeping changes in board processes, engaged faculty members more fully in governance, and by all accounts emerged as an exemplary governing body. A board with able leadership can bring about positive change in a crisis.

Other change-adept boards skillfully exploit what Richard Chait, a professor at the Harvard Graduate School of Education and a governance expert, calls "points of entry," those moments that present the board with the opportunity and the obligation to take decisive action. Sometimes opportunities occur at times of presidential transition. Widener University's board reversed the university's well-entrenched isolation from its community when it hired an experienced champion of civic engagement as president. Agnes Scott College's board sought a new president who would build the student body and revitalize the educational program.

At other times, leadership heeds subtle warnings that change is essential to prevent crisis, as when the board and the president of Northern Kentucky University realized that only comprehensive operational change would allow the university to sustain its momentum in spite of reduced state financial support. Where appropriate, these boards engaged the larger campus community—including faculty members and other stakeholders—in understanding, shaping, and implementing the change.

2. Adopt high aspirations for the institution, the president, and the board.

Great boards set high expectations for the institutions they govern, their presidents, and themselves as boards. The three components are inseparable. "To be a really successful president requires a highly effective board," commented an especially able public university president. Noted his board chair: "We simply could not achieve what we must for this university and this region without a top-notch president."

Failure to achieve the highest potential begins with a failure of imagination. No one sets out to strive for mediocrity, but implicitly many board members assume that the way things are dictates the way things must be—that they and their college can't do much better. "She is probably as good as we can get," surmised one board chair in weighing the college's chances of replacing an erratic president with a better one. Another board had become so accustomed to lurching from one financial crisis to another that it could not imagine a stable pattern of steady growth.

The crucial difference between a stagnant institution and one on an upward trajectory is the board's and the president's capacity to envision a better future and do the hard work to make that vision a reality. As one veteran board member puts it, "good enough is the worst enemy of the best." Aspirations among the colleges and universities described in this book include becoming a premier Hispanic-serving institution, an excellent public metropolitan university, an exceptional natural-health-care university, an exemplary public liberal arts college, and a leading regional university. But high hopes are not enough. Bold aspirations must be supported by the pedestrian, but vital and often difficult, work of planning, relationship building, fund raising, and the rest.

3. Align the work of the board with the institution's top priorities and change agenda.

Whether change involves radical transformation or steady, purposeful improvement, it occurs best when an institution's initiatives align with its aspirations. This convergence of priorities and actions must include the work of the board. In the fiercely competitive world of higher education, boards must focus on two questions: Is the institution financially and educationally healthy? Is it moving purposefully toward higher quality, greater effectiveness, and a stronger competitive position? When it comes to improving at the institutional level, high-functioning boards insist that governance structures, practices, and performance support affirmative answers to these questions. They ensure that the board's focus of attention, time on task, committee structure and assignments, agenda setting, and board members' own learning all contribute to change.

Some boards use targeted committee work to align board attention with institutional priorities. When Widener University adopted civic engagement as the cornerstone in its transformation, the board set up a new committee on civic engagement with a nationally known expert in the field as its chair. Northwestern Health Sciences University vowed in its revised mission to become a nationally recognized exemplar of integrated health, and the board also created a committee to champion this cause. Agnes Scott College used board task forces on marketing, financial aid, and enrollment to tackle the college's problem of declining enrollment. These task forces brought faculty members, administrators, and board members together to focus on this priority.

The best boards incorporate their own performance into the change formula. They pay close attention to their proficiency at governance, and they rigorously evaluate their own individual and collective performance. Inevitably, a great board has a talented chair working with a cadre of engaged board members, but every member feels personally committed to the work of the board and to advancing the institution. As one board member put it, "the Yankees don't go on the field with only five players who really want to win." Most of the institutions described in this book benefited from board leadership that inspired all board members to dedicated action.

4. Attract, support, and reward able presidents who are prepared to lead change, while observing their performance over time.

The best boards take great pains to attract the most-able presidents. Boards that seek to bring change take great pains to attract presidents who are themselves skilled at leading change and adroit at managing the opposition that change inevitably brings. Such boards expect a lot of their executives and make sure that they receive the support they need to make leadership prosper. These boards take charge of the search process, as a crucial turning point, to seek the best possible match between the fundamental aspirations of the institution and the capacities of the new executive. That leadership role includes engaging major constituents—especially faculty members—in setting criteria and giving their opinion on candidates. The board may turn to search experts who will take the time to learn what the campus is about and conduct penetrating interviews and background checks. But at the end of the day, the board ensures that the institution's long-term interests prevail over the immediate desires of any single group, however valued.

A number of the change-adept boards described in this book looked first in their own backyards in their search for a new president. American University, Hendrix College, Johnson & Wales University, the University of Dubuque, and the University of Wisconsin System all found able leaders among their own ranks, and the University System of Maryland persuaded a former president of the state flagship to return as the system's leader.

Other thoughtful boards looked to outsiders who had actually accomplished the kind of change they wanted to introduce. The College of New Jersey, which sought private-college quality at public-college prices, found one new president at a superior public institution and his successor at a notable independent university. The board at Agnes Scott College also looked outside the institution, but it was able to move more slowly and deliberately by hiring an experienced leader as interim president between a retiring president and a new one. Board members at Metropolitan State College of Denver could have hired a competent president quickly, but they spent two years finding the person who could build the kind of exceptional institution they envisioned.

The best boards wear bifocals with respect to the president. They stand close to him or her and remain supportive. Yet, at the same time, they take a longer view in realizing that the relationship will not last forever. Such boards use regular presidential performance evaluations to establish clear expectations, mutual priorities, and appropriate board oversight.

Most successful presidencies run through three stages: from the first few years of fresh achievements and growing confidence, to a middle period of effective service from a leader who knows the territory and whose early initiatives are bearing fruit, to the final stage when major projects come to a successful close. The board must be alert to transition points, provide the right doses of support, encouragement, and admonitions, and then plan for (and when necessary require) the president's departure.

Board members and presidents who enjoy a mutually respectful and supportive relationship also conduct conversations about when and how the relationship will end. The University of Northern Kentucky board and its president periodically discuss the succession process, though at this writing neither party feels the need to set a date. More commonly, board members avoid this difficult conversation until too late in the performance. The conversation about the end of the play should begin well before the last act. Once broached, it usually comes as a relief to everyone at the table.

5. Respect the equilibrium of governance by honoring responsibilities and boundaries, even while remaining deeply engaged in guiding change.

Genuinely change-adept boards achieve and manage equilibrium in the processes and practices of governance. The equilibrium of governance comes into play in the board's relationship with the president and administration, as well as in board members' interactions with one another. Without undermining the president's real authority or credibility, the board must ensure that the administration is doing its job to accomplish the mission and vision. This equilibrium also includes understanding shared governance and defining the relationship between the board and faculty. Within the board, policies should be in place to delineate the roles, responsibilities, and expectations of board members and to protect against conflicts between personal and institutional interests. It takes special board vigilance to avoid micromanaging change and to maintain governance equilibrium.

The line between policy setting and management often becomes clear only after it has been breached. Especially in the midst of change, engaged board members sometimes hover around this boundary, but the best boards recognize when they violate the border and retreat. Opinions among governance experts differ on whether a crisis or scandal justifies a temporary incursion into management territory. One veteran board member's experience leads him to say that assuming the reins of management will distract the board from its chief duties and probably result in poor management, too.

Negotiating the balance between management and administration can be especially delicate at smaller, less affluent institutions where the lawyer on the board is asked to render legal advice and the insurance executive is asked to estimate risk. The Oberlin College board became especially skilled at defining boundaries so that it is clear what decisions belong to the board, to the administration, and to the faculty. When it comes to governance, one board member says, "The board needs to police itself." All board members should learn what is expected of them in terms of attendance, preparation for meetings, and committee service. The best boards discuss and develop rules of engagement so that there are no misunderstandings about responsibilities and boundaries.

Well-informed debate and dissent are essential to robust and engaged governance that gets change right. The negativity of dissent should not sour the whole group, of course. One governance committee chair believes that disagreement is beneficial as long as it does not reflect a personal agenda, remains fact-based, and the chair informs the dissenter when "enough is enough." Laughter is a defining feature of the board and committee meetings of high-functioning boards. In the less-formal committee environment, board members are attentive, but conversation is lively. Divergent views are welcomed, and there is no shortage of repartee. A remarkable number of committed board members in these institutions report that meetings are fun, even in the midst of notable change. Governance need not be deadly serious.

6. Evaluate and reflect on individual and collective performance, as well as support for change; then make the right choices.

The best boards use individual and collective evaluation to self-diagnose, obtain an outsider's opinion on their functional health, and use what they learn to improve their governance process and practices so that they can make better choices on the institution's behalf. Diagnosis of their performance in guiding and supporting positive change is part of this self-reflection. It's good to have assistance from an objective outsider who can assess not just how the board thinks it is performing, but also how other stakeholders regard the board's performance.

Board self-appraisal can be a rewarding process with positive outcomes. One large state university, which does not reflect the trend among its public peers, describes its periodic internal review "like a family council," where the board can clear the air on its performance and any hot topics that bedevil board members at the moment. The review involves a comprehensive questionnaire administered every three years, followed by an all-day retreat to discuss the results.

Especially for institutions that are moving in a different direction or that have just weathered a significant transition, board self-assessment can be an especially productive way to take stock of current board performance and identify priorities for appropriate next steps. The objective opinion of an outside consultant can help a board discuss problems and take steps to remedy them. Board self-appraisal is akin to an annual physical, which the patient schedules whether or not something is amiss. The internist's diagnostic process includes a review of last year's test results, questions about new symptoms, and the results of blood pressure, heart rate, and blood tests. The doctor may recommend new medication or a change in living habits, but the outcome may also be to stay on the same course. The trick is to find the right internist.

Before its governance overhaul, the Johnson & Wales University board asked an outside consultant to conduct a personal interview with every board member on the quality of his or her own performance and that of the whole board. The results, along with recommendations for change, were reported to the governance committee. The committee accepted some of the advice, including the adoption of term limits—a particularly anguishing decision since it meant that some long-serving and well-liked trustees would be asked to leave the board.

7. Attract and develop each board member with an eye toward his or her potential for change leadership and deepen his or her personal commitment to the institution and its values.

The AGB report's findings on board recruitment and selection confirm that great board members are getting harder to find.[17] While most colleges and universities can attract the kinds of individuals they need, one-quarter of private institutions and one-fifth of publics find that more potential board members turn them down more than in the past. The reasons are understandable. The most sought-after people are busy, their philanthropic commitments are substantial, and they are concerned about accountability and transparency in the world after Sarbanes-Oxley. Political interference keeps some would-be public board members away, while state laws requiring public disclosure of assets deter others. However, offering potential new trustees the opportunity to make important changes in the life of the institution is one way to encourage them to overcome whatever hesitancy they have. The lure of making a real difference is especially attractive to those with experience in leading complex business or nonprofit organizations. Such people are often also adept at bringing change in a competitive environment as well.

The best boards know that being a talent magnet is the foundation of high performance, and they do everything they can to attract the most-able individuals. These boards assess current board capabilities to learn what they need in new members, recruit people who fit those needs, find ways to intrigue them with the institution's mission, and eventually instill a sense of commitment if it does not already exist. Nurturing commitment may be more difficult for less prestigious or less affluent institutions that seek non-alumni members. These boards often point to a larger social purpose—quality education, civic engagement, social progress—for serving.

Recruitment is also complicated for institutions that have experienced a recent crisis. After the board of American University virtually disintegrated when the chair and many members resigned, the board seized the opportunity to rebuild. Knowing they needed credibility and a deep understanding of higher education, they recruited board members with those strengths.

---

[17] *Policies, Practices, and Composition of Governing Boards of Public Colleges and Universities* (AGB Press, 2010).

Public university boards and presidents exert more influence over the selection of new members than most realize. As noted in Chapter 6, nearly three-quarters of public institutions report having at least some influence over who joins their board, according to the AGB study. State governors appoint most public boards, though in Michigan, Nebraska, and Nevada, trustees run for election. Ohio leavens its public boards with "national" members, a practice worth imitating. Often a well-connected public board chair and political donors on the board can sway a governor's choices. With producing more and better prepared graduates in less time a major priority in many states, governors can be encouraged to appoint trustees who will work with their executives to bring about these improvements.

Changing the Change Maker

"We cannot become what we need to be by remaining what we are."

—MAX DEPREE, *Leadership Is an Art* (Crown Business, 2004)

The boards and presidents at the institutions profiled in this book would no doubt agree that the process of change has changed them personally, as well as their colleges and universities. In the heat of change, they have focused appropriately on their aspirations for the institution and on the ultimate destination: a higher level of performance, defined in a multitude of ways. But the act of creating institutional change often prompts or even forces positive individual shifts in thinking and behavior.

We began this book with the observation that effective change leaders—boards and presidents—are engaged with their institutions and with one another, comfortable with the unpredictability of change, and astute and committed practitioners of their roles. Although we have shown how their leadership alters the "destination," it is useful to remember that change also alters its makers, giving them a deeper understanding of the responsibilities and satisfactions of board service, a stronger commitment to their institutions and to higher education in general, rewarding relationships with one another, and—most important—a great sense of personal accomplishment for having collectively affected students' lives and futures. Change that changes both the destination and the maker is indeed change for the better.

APPENDIX: CASE STUDIES

AGNES SCOTT COLLEGE

Featured in Chapter 8

2011 Profile

Location:	Decatur, Ga.
Enrollment:	900 undergraduate
Classification:	Private women's, baccalaureate
Operating Budget:	$46.5 million
Endowment:	$235 million
Board Members:	31

Quick Facts

- The college's founding is tied to the Presbyterian Church, and that tie continues today. The Board of Trustees must include a significant number who are members of the Presbyterian Church in the United States—at least two of whom shall be ordained Ministers of Word and Sacrament—while also reflecting the diversity of the campus community.

- Located in the Atlanta metropolitan area, the college is an attractive traditional southern campus distinguished by its "American collegiate Gothic" architecture. The campus is listed in the National Register of Historic Places and ranks high the Princeton Review's list of "most beautiful campuses." It has been immortalized in such movies as *A Man Called Peter, The Four Seasons, Scream 2,* and *The Blind Side.*

- This private liberal arts college has a reputation for high academic standards, evidenced by its Phi Beta Kappa chapter and its ranking in the top 10 percent of American colleges whose graduates complete Ph.D. degrees. *U.S. News & World Report* ranks it #2 among 2011 "Up and Comers" for promising and innovative changes.

- The college is a diverse community of scholars with more than 40 percent of degree-seeking undergraduates students of color, 10 percent international, and 43 percent Pell recipients. Students come from 43 states and U.S. territories and 37 countries.

- The most academically qualified students receive an Agnes Advantage Award at the time of their admission to the college. These $3,000 awards may be used for study abroad, mentored research opportunities, or internship experiences upon completion of the sophomore year. About 40 percent of graduates study abroad and 60 percent complete at least one internship.

Summary of Change

In the early 1990s, the board of Agnes Scott faced a run of serious challenges to the college's future, most notably declining enrollment and strained faculty relations. The central question was whether Agnes Scott had become too small to be viable.

While enrollment had declined, there had been no corresponding decrease in academic programs, resulting in a curriculum and faculty designed for a college twice its size. Alumnae trustees knew that enrollment had dropped, and seeing other women's colleges closing or admitting men to address enrollment problems, they began to wonder what the future would hold for their alma mater. One board member expressed concern that, during this troubled period, "the college had lost some of its competitive edge." Another board member speculated that "the college might close in several decades, or fade off, or shift its mission."

Agnes Scott had an impressive endowment that placed it among the top institutions in the nation for endowment per student. However, the college's interpretation of the bequest that provided the largest portion of the endowment restricted spending from it. Furthermore, it had no formal endowment-spending policy, which reinforced a practice of not spending. At one point, the college's auditors called Agnes Scott "an endowment with a college on the side."

Relations between the board and the faculty were also strained. Referring to "the bad old days," one faculty member described the board as aloof from the faculty and said that the faculty had a low regard for the board. In the early 1990s, a faculty vote of no confidence in the president got the board's attention. A former board chair said the vote "was a galvanizer, but the board was ready to be galvanized."

While the board publicly supported the president, they also worked behind the scenes to make her departure as graceful as possible. They employed an interim president before hiring a visionary alumna, Mary Brown Bullock, who served as president from 1995 through 2006, for the permanent job. Meanwhile, a board transition took place, too. Under a new board chair's leadership, the board began to be populated by "more tough-minded alumnae who wouldn't accept anything second rate," said one former trustee.

The evolving board composition brought changes to the board's structure and operation, including the establishment of term limits. Among the other changes was the creation of an endowment-spending policy that put that institutional asset to the use for which it was created: education. In addition, the board spent several years understanding and testing the limits of the bequest, which had great control over the institution's spending from a large gift of Coca-Cola stock. Those actions altered the board's perspective on the maintenance and distribution of the endowment.

To achieve Mary Brown Bullock's vision for a student body of 1,000, the board focused on marketing the college, increasing the tuition discount to 60 percent, and rebuilding the campus. As a result, first-year enrollment grew rapidly, nearly doubling by Bullock's second year. When she retired, the college had exceeded the 1,000-student goal. During this time, the board also worked on clarifying the duties of the faculty and the board and, according to one board member, the two groups "gradually worked to a more collegial relationship." The board also spent time improving its own practices, moving intentionally from a caretaking board to an engaged board doing "true board work."

AMERICAN UNIVERSITY

Featured in Chapter 2

2011 Profile

Location:	Washington, D.C.
Enrollment:	6,800 undergraduate; 5,700 postgraduate; 500 visiting
Classification:	Private, doctoral
Operating Budget:	$479 million
Endowment:	$433 million
Board Members:	33

Quick Facts

- American has six major schools and colleges: arts and sciences, business, communication, international service, law, and public affairs.

- Since 2006, students have been recognized twice by Princeton Review as the most politically active in the nation.

- With almost 1,900 international-studies majors, the School of International Service is the largest undergraduate program in the country.

- More than 80 percent of undergraduates and 60 percent of graduate students participate in at least one internship or other experiential education program.

Summary of Change

Chartered by Congress in 1893, American University consistently receives high rankings for academic programs in public affairs, law, and international service; student quality of life; and political activism. But public attention shifted in 2005 and 2006 to the castigation that the board of trustees received from Senate Finance Committee Chairman Charles Grassley (R-IA). After public whistleblower allegations that then-President Benjamin Ladner had been using university funds improperly, Grassley threatened federal legislation mandating changes in board structure, composition, and governance. Fortunately, American took the right steps to correct its mistakes and avoid federal involvement. The changes and their consequences speak more to a board turnaround than to an institutional turnaround, and the story portrays a board of trustees that has a tremendous impact on its university.

While the board's problems may have had deep roots, they grew visible when the board sought outside advice on executive compensation. After consultants reported that Ladner's salary—always at the high end for his peer group—could be considered excessive, the board approved a 16 percent reduction in April 2005. Not surprisingly, the president disagreed with this decision.

Meanwhile, in March of that year, the board had received an anonymous letter alleging Ladner's improper use of funds. Following an investigation, the audit committee recommended that the university report an additional $400,000 in executive compensation to the IRS and demand reimbursement from the president for $125,000 plus interest in personal expenses. In August, the executive committee suspended Ladner. Two months later the whole board accepted the audit committee's recommendations, terminated Ladner's contract, and reached a settlement in a contentious buyout.

But American's biggest problem was its broken board. As Thomas A. Gottschalk, former vice chair and interim chair of the board explained, Ladner was "a victim of his own success. And, trustees were victims of his success, too. It made them too passive. Our greatest virtue became our greatest vice."

This board meltdown surfaced other deeply embedded flaws in the governance structure: insufficient oversight, an inside/outside board, a strong executive committee insulated from the rest of the board, and board isolation from campus—particularly faculty—opinion. Appropriate policies were in place for conflicts of interest, campus representatives, and board member responsibilities, but they were not followed.

When the board chair resigned without notice in October 2005, Gary Abramson was elected chair. Provost Neil Kerwin was named interim president (and later permanent president). Following a wholesale self-study of current governance structures and an investigation of potential areas for improvement, a special governance committee recommended 34 changes in 20 areas of governance.

Recognizing how important it was for the board to regain credibility in higher education, the faculty made a compelling case for healing the board and the campus. There was extensive dialogue between the faculty and board committees. An ad hoc committee on governance reform appointed by the faculty senate recommended 15 action items, including greater transparency, faculty participation, and oversight. The board adopted most of those recommendations.

Because there was an inside/outside board, the board had not been able to agree on how to handle the crisis. When Benjamin Ladner left, the dissent continued, and several board members resigned. In recruiting new members, the board intentionally sought credibility and expertise in higher education and accountability. New board members included a former director of the Peace Corps and two former college presidents.

The crisis did not affect giving, enrollment, applications, or any other meaningful indicator of institutional performance. In fact, as former Director of Institutional Research Elizabeth Sibolski noted, "As trust and confidence is restored in the institution, people are willing to help." A capital campaign proceeded uninterrupted. Faculty members now have a more intentional link to leadership through their board representatives. The board has been reunited and re-energized.

After the dust settled, the board, president, and senior administrative team completed a new strategic plan, adopted by the board in 2008. Finally, a spirit of openness and transparency permeates the campus, evidenced by enhanced communications, including a board of trustees section on the university's award-winning Web site, two town hall meetings a year with the president and the board chair, presentations by deans and faculty members on a rotating basis during meetings of the whole board, student and faculty nonvoting members of the board, and faculty members on all committees. The strategic plan, Neil Kerwin says, is "both a symbolic and practical end of board renewal."

HENDRIX COLLEGE

Featured in Chapter 4

2011 Profile

Location:	Conway, Ark.
Enrollment:	1,468 undergraduate
Classification:	Private, master's
Operating Budget:	$64 million
Endowment:	$175 million
Board Members:	40

Quick Facts

- Tuition at Hendrix runs $41,000, including room and board, with an average discount rate of 60 percent. The high-tuition/high-discount formula is a strategic one.

- Roughly half of Hendrix's students come from beyond Arkansas, and all are well prepared. Incoming students have an average GPA of 3.76; ACT scores average 27.8, and SAT scores are typically in the mid-1200s. Retention and graduation rates approach those of other well-regarded Midwestern liberal arts colleges.

- The science program at Hendrix is historically strong, with 40 percent of students majoring in the sciences. An estimated one in eight physicians in Arkansas graduated from Hendrix.

- Hendrix is affiliated with the United Methodist church. Its bylaws require the 40-member board of trustees to include five United Methodist clergy from Arkansas and five United Methodist lay leaders or clergy from outside the state.

Summary of Change

Until the early 1990s, Hendrix College occupied a comfortable niche as one of the region's best liberal arts colleges. In *Colleges that Change Lives* (Penguin, 2006), Loren Pope describes the 50-acre campus, adjacent to a sleepy town, as a "Shangri-la in Conway, Arkansas" and rates it "one of the country's academic gems."

In 2001 and 2002, Hendrix faced a looming financial crisis. First, the state trimmed significantly a key scholarship program, in effect making Hendrix a more expensive, private option. Second, the Walton Foundation gave the University of Arkansas in Fayetteville $300 million to create its Honors College and improve its academic programs and reputation. Finally, the events of September 11, 2001, caused a decline in foreign-student enrollment and drove down the value of Hendrix's endowment. The college could have weathered any one of these threats without dramatic change, but the three in combination demanded a sweeping overhaul.

On September 11, the Hendrix board was interviewing new presidential candidates. It selected J. Timothy Cloyd, then vice president for development and college relations, who held a doctorate in political science and had taught at Vanderbilt University. Since then, the story has been one of a highly engaged board working closely with an entrepreneurial president to meet the demands of the crisis and use it as a springboard to advance Hendrix as a national leader in liberal arts and sciences education.

What makes a relatively small liberal arts college with high tuition in a non-destination town successful? Part of the answer lies in its two most distinctive academic programs: the sciences and the Odyssey program. Science has been a strong point of the curriculum for many years. More recently, Hendrix established the Odyssey Program to provide an exciting curricular and co-curricular experience. The brainchild of the current president, this program requires all students to engage in experiences that are approved and mentored by the faculty in three of the following six areas: artistic creativity, global awareness, professional leadership development, service to the world, undergraduate research, and special projects. The program defines the Hendrix experience and differentiates the college.

Hendrix developed this program with the explicit intention of strengthening its competitiveness in the market for students. Hendrix needed to raise tuition 25 percent. Without an additional signature academic program, the college feared a drop in enrollment of qualified students or pressure to lower admissions standards.

Hendrix is also breaking ground on a new kind of town-gown relationship. The college owned 160 acres next to the campus that was used as a forested science lab and an outdoor space for students and local residents. The board considered selling the property, but it wanted to retain control over the character of the development. Timothy Cloyd, with board support, engaged Andres Duany of Duany-Plater Zyberk (the firm that created Seaside, Fla.) to develop a plan for the Village at Hendrix, as a new urban "walkable community" that combines academic space with residential and business development. The project enlivens the physical environment around the campus, and it may also net more than $80 million. Because this real-estate venture has raised concerns about whether it draws too much energy and attention away from this Methodist college's liberal arts mission, the board created a for-profit LLC to manage the project. The five-member Village at Hendrix LLC board is chaired by a board member with experience in real estate. The college also hired a CEO with experience developing and managing similar endeavors.

A sampling of statistics suggests that Hendrix is on a marked upward trajectory. Applications, campus visits, and enrollment are all up by more than 15 percent. Net tuition continues to rise every quarter. The college successfully completed an ambitious capital campaign that raised $101.3 million, surpassing its $100 million goal. And Hendrix has been featured in national media, including the *New York Times, Chicago Tribune, Miami Herald,* and *Los Angeles Times.*

JOHNSON & WALES UNIVERSITY

Featured in Chapter 6

2011 Profile

Location:	Headquartered in Providence, R.I. with regional campuses in North Miami, Fla.; Denver, Colo.; and Charlotte, N. C.
Enrollment:	17,000
Classification:	Private, doctorate
Operating Budget:	$288 million
Endowment:	$214 million
Board Members:	18

Quick Facts

- Founded as a business school in 1914, Johnson & Wales has evolved from a proprietary school to a university. In 1963, JWU was awarded nonprofit status and chartered to award associate degrees. Seven years later, the state extended degree-granting authority to the baccalaureate level, and in 1980 the university was authorized to award graduate degrees.

- In 1984, JWU established its first branch campus in Charleston, S.C. Throughout the next two decades, it expanded to campuses and other teaching locations in Norfolk, Va. (1986); North Miami, Fla. (1992); Worcester, Mass. (1992); Vail (1993) and Denver (2001), Colo.; Gothenburg, Sweden (1994); and Charlotte, N.C. (2004). Several of these locations were subsequently closed, and JWU made a strategic decision to consolidate some of its smaller campuses.

- JWU now enrolls students in its College of Business, College of Culinary Arts, and The Hospitality College, all programs with international reputations; School of Technology; School of Arts & Sciences; Graduate School; and School of Education, at its Providence campus. Many of these programs also available at its regional campuses. JWU is considered one of the largest food-service educators in the world.

- The current board consists of professionals from large corporations, higher education, and the nonprofit sector, including Chef Emeril Lagasse '78, chef, and television personality; James Hance Jr., former vice chairman and chief financial officer of Bank of America; William E. Trueheart, chief executive officer of Achieving the Dream: Community Colleges Count, and former college president; and Guy Snowden, director of SnowMark Corporation, a venture-capital firm.

Summary of Change

The Johnson & Wales University board of trustees consisted of members connected to the university's last owner when it was a proprietary institution. Under the leadership of Chair John A. Yena, a former JWU president, and with the guidance of a consultant, the university committed to a major governance transformation. After thoughtful research, board leaders introduced changes to the board's composition and structure by instituting term limits, formal board member assessments, orientation sessions for new trustees, a special status for "legacy trustees," and a board-recruitment process based on institutional needs rather than personal relationships.

These board changes were difficult, especially given the strong and long-standing personal connections of board members. While some former board members remained friends of the institution, others felt betrayed. The new board included both continuing board members and newcomers, including leaders from various industries, like Don W. Hubble, an experienced corporate executive who chaired the committee that championed the shift to a modern governance structure. In the midst of the board transformation, the next JWU president was appointed. A change in attitude was an intended consequence of this leadership transition: The board became more independent.

The two most important contributions of this newly empowered board were a new emphasis on educational quality and greater investment in institutionally funded financial aid. At the suggestion of the board, the newly appointed president, John J. Bowen '77, developed a five-year strategic plan (FOCUS 2011) that sought to improve selectivity, educational quality, affordability, and the student experience at the university by curtailing enrollment growth, improving the university's retention rate, and committing more funds to institutional financial aid in efforts to reduce the average student debt. Other qualitative improvements included strengthening the faculty, reviewing all and bolstering key academic programs, and enhancing the physical plant.

For an institution as focused on fiscal stability as JWU was, these were risky moves. John Bowen readily admits that he would not have pursued them if the board members had not insisted. Today, JWU is as strong financially as ever and more successful in moving students to graduation and careers in a reasonable period of time. It is also enabling its graduates—many from moderate and low-income families—to graduate without crushing debt. In spite of all the changes, the university has continued to net an average of $38 million from operations over the span of FOCUS 2011, which is a source of continued financial strength and a basis for continued positive change.

METROPOLITAN STATE COLLEGE OF DENVER

Featured in Chapter 5

2011 Profile

Location:	Denver, Colo. (downtown and other locations)
Enrollment:	21,000
Classification:	Public, master's
Operating Budget:	$106 million
Endowment:	$8 million
Board Members:	9 voting members

Quick Facts

- Best known by its nickname, Metro Denver, Metropolitan State College of Denver is very much an urban institution. It hosts a Center for Urban Education to prepare teachers for city schools; an Urban Leadership Program to nurture political, community, and business leaders; and a Center for Urban Connections to support service-learning opportunities for students.

- Fully 80 percent of Metro State's more than 67,500 alumni live and work in the greater Denver area.

- In a unique shared-campus environment, Metro State shares a downtown campus known as Auraria Higher Education Center with the University of Colorado-Denver and Community College of Denver.

- Students of color make up 28 percent of enrollment. Metro State ranks in the top 100 institutions in the nation for graduating students of color.

- The college sets high and highly visible aspirations. It aims to become "the preeminent public urban baccalaureate institution in the nation" and seeks the status of Hispanic Serving Institution (HSI), which would require 25 percent Hispanic enrollment and make Metro eligible for additional federal funding.

Summary of Change

In 2002, Colorado Governor Bill Owens signed a law dissolving a four-campus system that included three smaller rural campuses and Metropolitan State College of Denver. Each institution received its own board of trustees. The Metro State Foundation board had been strong advocates for independence and fully expected that members of the new campus-based governing boards would be drawn from its ranks. Instead, the governor appointed others, including business executive and entrepreneur Bruce D. Benson, who was the first board chair. Benson led a two-year presidential search that resulted in the appointment of Denver native Stephen M. Jordan, president of Eastern Washington University and rising star among regional university presidents. The board expected Jordan to work with them in leading change and increasing the profile of Metro State in the Denver area. They have not been disappointed.

Many board members are Denver business, political, or civic leaders, and frequently all three. The board culture prizes high aspirations for the college, the board, and the president: becoming preeminent and Hispanic serving; maintaining a lean administration, low operating costs, and modest tuition; creating public-private partnerships rather than relying on public support; developing metrics to document achievement; and taking an evidence-based approach to evaluating new and continuing programs. Board members are profoundly supportive of Jordan's leadership style, yet they regularly challenge his proposals and put forward change ideas of their own.

Two signature initiatives that illustrate a vibrant board-president relationship are the board-initiated pay-for-performance plan for faculty compensation and the new Hotel and Hospitality Learning Center (HLC). The pay-for-performance initiative—deferred when the recession led to sharp state reductions in the operating budget—would have linked faculty pay more closely to peer assessments of their performance and other criteria than the across-the-board model that was in place. Following a sometimes tense series of conversations among faculty leaders, board members, and the president, all parties came to agreement on an approach to faculty pay that recognized teaching performance.

The Hotel and Hospitality Learning Center, to be operated by the Marriott Corporation, is intended as a learning site for students studying hotel, hospitality, and tourism management and as a source of net revenue to the Metro State Foundation to build the college's endowment. Energetic board members were intimately involved in this project. Their roles included facilitating the assembly of the right players, including public officials and Marriott representatives, and lending their expertise in urban land development, finance, and the legalities of this complicated relationship.

In summing up the board's attitude toward its entrepreneurial president and change, Adele Phelan, the former chair, observed: "We don't always agree with Steve at the start, but we trust him and usually agree to his proposals provided there is solid accountability. We know that failure sometimes accompanies risk, but we believe that risk is good."

NORTHERN KENTUCKY UNIVERSITY

Featured in Chapter 2

2011 Profile

Location:	Highland Heights, KY, a suburb of Cincinnati
Enrollment:	15,748, including 1,500 graduate and 600 law students
Classification:	Public, doctoral
Operating budget:	$200 million
Endowment:	$54 million
Board Members:	11

Quick Facts

- Growth in size and quality mark the NKU change story. In the decade ending in 2010, graduates in the STEM disciplines of science, technology, engineering, and mathematics more than doubled, while in the same period minority graduates jumped a remarkable 230 percent. There has been a 72 percent increase in degrees produced over the past decade.

- New construction includes a $60-million basketball arena, Bank of Kentucky Center, which dominates one entrance to the campus. A $37-million student union opened recently, and Griffin Hall, a new facility for the College of Informatics, is in progress.

- Only about a quarter of the university's operating budget comes from the state. Tuition and fees generate 60 percent.

- The region—a sprawling three-county residential, business, and industrial band just south of Cincinnati—is one of the state's most important economic engines, sometimes overlooked by political forces in the state capitol of Frankfort.

Summary of Change

Northern Kentucky University is in the front rank of urban or metropolitan institutions that aspire to become the premier metropolitan universities or colleges in their regions. With its large commuter population, applied programs that feed the local job market, an educational philosophy of community engagement, and a genuine commitment to serving economic and social needs, it is enmeshed in this rapidly growing part of Kentucky. NKU's impressive business plan supports the region's aim of adding 50,000 jobs and $270 million in new state revenue annually and makes the case that investing in the university will pay dividends quickly. Institutional change is focused on how the university can sustain its momentum in a new era of significantly reduced state support, changing enrollment patterns and demographics, and emerging technology that influences the teaching-learning process.

The major driver of change at NKU is the high-functioning relationship between a long-serving board and a very able president. Both agree that a successful president requires a strong board, and a highly effective board requires a highly effective president and administration. With an energetic president like James C. Votruba, many boards would yield to the temptation to let the executive dominate the relationship. But this board ensures the right equilibrium by remaining actively engaged, particularly at the strategic level.

One feature of high-performing boards is their deliberate care in matching institutional needs with presidential leadership skills. Jim Votruba and NKU have been a good match. After 14 years, the board openly discusses what the university will need in his successor, although no departure date has been set and the board remains pleased with his performance.

NORTHWESTERN HEALTH SCIENCES UNIVERSITY

Featured in Chapter 6

2011 Profile

Location:	Bloomington, Minn.
Enrollment:	1,029
Classification:	Private, master's
Operating Budget:	$25 million
Endowment:	$12 million
Board Members:	15

Quick Facts

- Founded in 1941 as Northwestern College of Chiropractic, an upper-division and graduate college, the institution changed its name in 1999 to Northwestern Health Sciences University. It added a massage therapy program in 2000, and in 2001, it acquired the Minnesota College of Acupuncture and Oriental Medicine.

- Applicants to the professional programs in chiropractic, Oriental medicine, and acupuncture must have earned 60 to 90 semester credits toward the baccalaureate degree. Graduate degrees require full-time study for eight to 10 trimesters. Massage therapy is a certificate program. The undergraduate program, enrolling about 150 students, awards the Bachelor of Science in human biology.

- Clinical research is a hallmark of the university. The program has garnered more than $15 million in federal research funding.

- A public clinic system receives more than 72,000 patient visits a year, making Northwestern the largest provider of natural health-care services in Minnesota. In addition, the university offers more than 150 internship sites in private-practice clinics.

Summary of Change

Between 1999 and 2001, the Northwestern College of Chiropractic acquired programs in massage therapy, acupuncture, and Oriental medicine as interesting opportunities to diversify the institution's program offerings. As the board and executive leadership worked to incorporate the programs, they also developed an appropriate new name, going from "chiropractic" to "health sciences" and from "college" to "university." The new focus on integrated health care originated in a 2005 board retreat. The board developed a position statement about the integrated model and then asked the administration to advance and implement it further.

At about this time, the board also initiated a search for a new president. Ultimately, it turned to one of Northwestern's own: an alumnus who had been on the board for eight years. Mark Zeigler was a practicing chiropractor who had served as mayor of Sturgis, S.D. He was hired primarily as a fund raiser, a role for which he is well suited. As Zeigler got to know the university from the inside, he learned that its leadership, facilities, and processes all required considerable attention to fulfill the new vision and get on track for greater success in recruiting students.

A major point of discussion among board members was whether the integrated model would include allopathic (traditional) medicine. Issues included how to address the tendency of traditional medicine to discount or place excessive limits on natural health-care practice, how the business model could work for diverse practitioners and for patients, and whether Northwestern's alumni were prepared to support this level of integration. The board and the president came to the conviction that "integrated" should include all health-care professions. They recognized that this approach would require significant cultural and operational changes in curriculum, clinics, alumni relations, and other areas.

Over the next two years, the new vision was a recurring board topic and the focus of a campus-wide integrative health-care committee. Despite considerable support, implementation was not on track. It proved challenging to develop an action plan because of the pioneering nature of the vision and the need to attend to other important issues simultaneously, including completing a major facilities campaign and restructuring the leadership team. With remarkable long-term persistence, the board and the president engaged a consultant to interview a cross-section of individuals and make recommendations for how to proceed. This exercise, along with a board retreat, strengthened the board's resolve and confidence while identifying the next steps.

One step was a process of planning and constituency engagement. Again with help from a consultant, the president and the board developed a strategic plan centered on the integrated health-care trajectory, with supportive scorecards for the university and the board. Focused planning, budgeting, and implementation have been helpful on all levels, the president reports, as evidenced by the recent establishment of a Center for Health Care Innovation and Policy as a focal point to help carry out the vision.

The transformation to integrated health care is a long-term process within the university and even longer in the world beyond. Northwestern continues to make steady progress with strong leadership from the president and the board. In addition to the new center, early indicators of progress include increased enrollment, emerging curriculum change, and a restructured leadership team that is ensuring steady progress while allowing the president more time to return to his fund-raising role.

OBERLIN COLLEGE

Featured in Chapter 3

2011 Profile

Location:	Oberlin, Ohio
Enrollment:	2,948 undergraduate
Classification:	Private, master's
Operating Budget:	$135 million
Endowment:	$659 million
Board Members:	34

Quick Facts

- The Oberlin Conservatory of Music, the oldest continuously operating conservatory in the United States, is located here. Students are admitted separately but can pursue degrees in both music and a traditional liberal arts subject via a five-year double-degree program.

- More Oberlin alumni earn Ph.D.'s than do alumni at any other liberal arts college in the country.

- Known for having a liberal or progressive student body, Oberlin was the nation's first coeducational college and the first to admit students regardless of race.

- A leader in the postsecondary-education sustainability movement, Oberlin has committed itself to becoming a climate-neutral campus, which includes achieving a net result of zero emissions of carbon dioxide, methane, and other greenhouse gases. An estimated 50 percent of electricity needs are met using sustainable energy sources.

- Along with the College of Wooster, Denison University, Kenyon College, and Ohio Wesleyan University, Oberlin is a member of the Five Colleges of Ohio consortium.

Summary of Change

For too many years, Oberlin's board had been "dominated by the issue du jour," according to one board member. Board members were reactive and involved in "very important details," not the organization as a whole. But after the tech bubble burst in 2001, and leading to three consecutive years of budget cuts, the board realized that practice was unsustainable. It had no planning tools in place to foresee the following year or years. Board members realized that they needed both a strategic plan and a strategic financial plan.

From 2003 to 2005, the board and the administration developed an understanding of Oberlin's business model and involved all campus constituencies in developing the strategic plan. For the first time, the strategic and financial plans were integrated. The financial plan's objectives and indicators have become the foundation of the board's work, informing every proposal, every agenda, and most discussions. Over the past five years, the college has made significant progress in consistent directions that everyone understands and supports. Because they recognize that it takes time to implement change, board members now rely on a long-term financial modeling tool that allows them to look three to 10 years ahead. The model gives the board confidence in its decisions.

Around the same time that budget cuts were occurring, the board and administration noticed a slow and steady decline in the percentage of admitted students who enrolled, so they commissioned a consultant to conduct a market-perception study. After learning that the perception of Oberlin was generic—more like a commodity than a brand—they made significant investments in branding and communications. Board members stepped up with personal gifts to help support the initiative.

The board also decided to trim back enrollment and reduce the endowment payout rate. These counterintuitive strategies to correct budget imbalances have paid huge dividends during the most recent downturn, in which Oberlin avoided layoffs and continued hiring for key positions, including tenure-track faculty. As a result, the college transformed the recovery energy into a long-term trajectory of continuous improvement.

The board took steps to improve its governance practices at the same time that it sought to reengineer the college's approach to financial sustainability. The board developed committees with clear charters and significant responsibilities. Committees are expected to revisit and possibly propose revisions to the charter and bylaws annually. The board uses a global working calendar for the year with indicators of success for each committee. Among the notable consequence of those changes are more-meaningful governance work, a dramatic increase in board giving, and a balance between board interest in academic or student issues and financial issues.

ROOSEVELT UNIVERSITY

Featured in Chapter 5

2011 Profile

Location:	Chicago, Ill.
Enrollment:	4,200 undergraduate; 3,100 graduate
Classification:	Private, doctoral
Operating Budget:	$114 million
Endowment:	$60.9 million
Board Members:	60

Quick Facts

- Roosevelt was founded as Thomas Jefferson College in 1945 and renamed later that same year in honor of Franklin D. Roosevelt. The college was rededicated to both Franklin and Eleanor Roosevelt in 1959. It maintains campuses in downtown Chicago and suburban Schaumburg.

- Student representatives are voting members of the university senate, and faculty members, alumni, and student representatives serve on the board of trustees. Members of the early advisory board included Marian Anderson, Pearl Buck, Ralph Bunche, Albert Einstein, Thomas Mann, Gunnar Myrdal, and Albert Schweitzer.

- The university includes the Chicago College of Performing Arts, a music and theater conservatory; the College of Arts and Sciences; the College of Education; the Evelyn T. Stone College of Professional Studies, a continuing education and professional-studies school; the College of Pharmacy; and the Walter E. Heller College of Business Administration.

- Roosevelt strives to admit residents of the inner city, students who work full time to support themselves, and students who are the first members of their families to attend college. A large percentage of Roosevelt students work either full time or part time.

- Roosevelt has a longstanding institutional commitment to social justice. It was ranked the 10th most diverse private university in America by the *New York Times* and the second most diverse in the Midwest by *U.S. News & World Report*.

Summary of Change

In the 1980s, Roosevelt was in a downward spiral, closing in on itself with inadequate funding, worn facilities, and moderate academic and professional standards. In 1988, a new president arrived with entrepreneurial energy and ideas that brought the university back from the brink. During the 1990s, a great deal was happening, but not all of it was effective or contributed to an appropriate and attractive image for the university. By the time the president left in 2002, the university needed a real strategic focus.

A key decision around that time was for Roosevelt to participate with DePaul University and Columbia College of Chicago in the joint management of the University Center of Chicago, a 1,670-bed residence hall to be constructed in the city. That led to the imperative to rethink the nature of the student body, especially in Chicago. In 2002, Roosevelt hired a new president, Charles R. Middleton, and developed a strategic plan. His approach has been to consolidate the gains and move forward systematically.

Today, both the board and the university are grounded in strategic goals, and that is a fundamental change for the university. The board has adopted a very purposeful approach to mission, image, metrics, and growth. James J. Mitchell III has chaired the board since 1994. Although Chuck Middleton has brought focus, the university's strategic objectives (2003) are intentionally broad concepts, not action plans. The board routinely uses the objectives routinely to place decisions and initiatives in context. Every board action and major discussion is explicitly tied to one or more goals.

The clarity of mission and strategies changed board and institutional dynamics. Chuck Middleton has been intentional about cultivating the board, which is especially important because of its large size (60 members). The board works hard to define and adhere to appropriate governance roles. During meetings, trustees gently call each other out about getting into the weeds. The executive committee has evolved from a strong decision-making body to a sounding board. Attendance at full board meetings is exceptional.

As the pace of change escalates, the magnitude of the decision rises. Chuck Middleton believes strongly that the board should make such decisions step by step, gaining comfort and confidence along the way.

THE COLLEGE OF NEW JERSEY

Featured in Chapter 8

2011 Profile

Location:	Ewing Township, N. J.
Enrollment:	6,460 undergraduate; 655 postgraduate
Classification:	Public, master's
Operating Budget:	$177 million
Endowment:	$18.5million
Board Members:	13

Quick Facts

- In the mid-1990s, Trenton State College, a teacher-preparation institution, changed its name and mission. The result was The College of New Jersey, a liberal arts college focused on residential undergraduate education. Ninety-five percent of students are from New Jersey.

- TCNJ's Georgian Colonial campus occupies 289 landscaped acres about five miles from the state capital of Trenton, 10 miles from Princeton, and one hour from Philadelphia and New York.

- Particularly well known for its preparation of teachers and highly selective biology program, *U.S. News & World Report* ranks The College of New Jersey as the top public regional university in the northern United States. TCNJ was named 10th in value in public higher education by the *Princeton Review* in 2009. In 2006, it was awarded a Phi Beta Kappa chapter—an honor shared by less than 10 percent of colleges and universities nationwide.

Summary of Change

Not many 140-year-old institutions get the chance for a complete transformation. The College of New Jersey (TCNJ) was founded in 1855 as the New Jersey State Normal School with a focus on training teachers. Over the next century, the school moved through various incarnations until becoming Trenton State College in 1958 and opening up to non-education majors in the following decade.

In a period of low enrollment during the 1970s, Peter Mills, the institution's chief financial officer, accurately predicted enrollment shortfalls due to the end of the Vietnam-era draft and the Baby Boom. He conceived of a "smaller but better" strategy as a practical alternative. Around the same time, Erna Hoover, a graduate of Harvard and Yale Universities, came on as board chair with the vision of transforming Trenton State into a public institution on a par with New Jersey's private institutions. As Mills and Hoover worked with President Clayton R. Brower and the other trustees, the new TCNJ was conceived.

Strong board leadership ushered TCNJ through the evolution from teacher's college to exceptional public institution. Through multiple presidents and changes in administrative leadership, the board has maintained its dedication to developing the institution by staying engaged in the college community and pursuing a shared vision for TCNJ. Trustees use their own professional expertise, ranging from medicine to finance to political influence, to advise and act on pertinent campus situations. Board meeting agendas, committee conversations, and retreat discussions all focus on making progress as a "national exemplar" of a selective residential institution known for the quality of its educational experience. There continues to be a disciplined convergence of attention around advancing the institution, whether the topic is a capital campaign, preserving relative independence from state regulation, a curriculum change, or faculty pay.

The board has leveraged its position to hire able administrative leaders who share the vision and have the talent to make it happen. Three presidents have led the school through its transition. Clayton Brower (1971–1980) took the risk of TCNJ becoming a smaller and better institution, and he engineered a special exception from New Jersey's funding formula to pay for the changes. Harold Eickhoff (1980–1999) fought to secure institutional autonomy, including an independent board of trustees for all of New Jersey's public colleges, separate from the statewide board. He also committed to the campus' Georgian mode of architecture. Perhaps more than any of her predecessors, R. Barbara Gitenstein (1999–present) has simultaneously strengthened the academic program, enhanced the shared governance structure, and bolstered TCNJ's reputation.

Given that TCNJ's vision is grounded in academics, the board recognized that the faculty was essential to any campuswide change. Without faculty buy-in, any transition plan would falter after leaving the boardroom. When Barbara Gitenstein arrived in 1999, faculty leaders presented her with a manifesto outlining what it would take to upgrade the academic program to meet incoming students' rising expectations. Faculty leaders were unhappy with the gap between the academic program and the experience their students sought. Barbara Gitenstein agreed. Over a record-breaking 18 months, she worked with the faculty on a wholesale transformation of the curriculum.

Since 1996, when the institution officially became The College of New Jersey, its reputation for academic excellence has grown. Average incoming SAT scores in 2010 were 1243, and one in three new students were in the top 5 percent of their high-school classes. Retention and graduation rates rival top private colleges and universities. Alumni satisfaction rates are close to 100 percent, with more than 95 percent of recent alums reporting they are in graduate school or working in their fields within a year of commencement. *U.S. News & World Report* has put TCNJ at the top of the public master's ranking for nearly 20 years. *Kiplinger's*, the *Fiske Guide*, and the *Princeton Review* also rank TCNJ highly. Its students regularly top the state Fundamentals of Engineering exam, CPA exam, nursing licensure exam, and the PraxisSeries test for future teachers. In only a few decades, TCNJ has been transformed from an average state college to a highly competitive public institution.

THUNDERBIRD SCHOOL OF GLOBAL MANAGEMENT

Featured in Chapter 4

2011 Profile

Location:	Glendale, Ariz.
Enrollment:	1,400
Classification:	Private, master's
Operating Budget:	$66 million
Endowment:	$15 million
Board Members:	33

Quick Facts

- Thunderbird is a graduate school focused exclusively on global business. It remains a leader in international business education, but it once was unique in this field. About half of its 1,400 students are enrolled in a full-time MBA program. Thunderbird also runs a thriving executive-education program with both standard and customized programs available in its residential setting.

- The board, faculty, and administration are rightly proud of the school's consistent number-one ranking in international business education by the *Financial Times, U.S. News & World Report,* and the *Wall Street Journal.*

- Thanks to its specialized mission and curriculum and its strong reputation, Thunderbird attracts board members with senior business experience and savvy. More than most colleges and universities, Thunderbird has what many presidents would call an activist board. It is populated by out-of-the-box thinkers, including many alumni, who are committed to success and not afraid of change.

Summary of Change

The Thunderbird School of Global Management, headquartered in Arizona, operates across Europe, South America, and Asia. Founded in 1946 on what had been Thunderbird Field, a World War II aviation training center, the campus' living and work spaces are converted barracks. A small air traffic control tower and the barracks lend special meaning to one of the school's guiding mantras: "Borders frequented by trade seldom need soldiers."

Thunderbird's name embodies singular excellence in global business education. By the 1990s, full-time enrollment had reached 1,400. In spite of a small endowment, the school supported a substantial cadre of well-compensated faculty, largely through tuition revenue. In this heady environment, the board "took a leap of faith" according to a former president, as it took on substantial new debt, banking on an enrollment hike of 200 students to meet the loan payments.

Several events conspired in the new century to threaten Thunderbird's hegemony and even its existence. First, domestic and international competition heated up in graduate business education. Thunderbird's success in global education attracted other players to the field. The Thunderbird brand and its top rankings partially insulated the school from its competitors, but as an observer close to the action put it, "Thunderbird was ahead of the crowd, but the crowd was galloping fast to catch up." Second, the pool of students pursuing graduate degrees in business began to shrink. Enrollment fell at Thunderbird as well. Then, in quick succession, the events of September 11, 2001, and the SARS epidemic in 2002 and 2003 led to a precipitous drop in enrollment, from 1,400 to 600.

Thunderbird faced an existential crisis. An enrollment free fall of more than 50 percent at a largely tuition-dependent institution with a limited endowment demanded quick action. The school would face difficulty in meeting its debt obligations at this reduced level of revenue. The usual response—across-the-board cuts; travel, purchasing, and hiring freezes; tuition hikes; and the like—would not come close to making a difference. Vertical cuts deep into the organization were essential to its survival. New revenue-generating services needed to be developed quickly, but there was little investment capital to underwrite new programs and no time for these programs to gain momentum in attracting students.

The board acted decisively to stem the cash hemorrhage and shore up the financial base. In concert with the administration, it reduced faculty from 120 to 40, largely among teachers of world languages. Remaining true to its global mission, Thunderbird began requiring a second language from all incoming students. To rebuild revenues, the board studied several alternatives before deciding to concentrate on executive education and graduate programs. In this process, trustees worked side by side with faculty members to develop the new programs and curricula. The board slowly gained the faculty's trust by sharing the realities that confronted the institution and by inviting them to play a lead role in making the tough decisions related to faculty reductions. Over time, this transparent process of inclusiveness contributed to the collaboration that helped reposition the institution.

The board restructured its debt and substantially reduced its annual debt costs. It hired a new president, Angel Cabrera, an internationally recognized business educator from Spain. Today, Thunderbird remains a going concern, although continually challenged by competition in the global education field that it pioneered.

TULANE UNIVERSITY

Featured in Chapter 4

2011 Profile

Location:	New Orleans, La.
Enrollment:	6,700 undergraduate; 4,400 postgraduate
Classification:	Private, doctoral
Operating Budget:	$785 million
Endowment:	$807.8 million
Board Members:	35

Quick Facts

- Founded in 1834 as the Medical College of Louisiana and later established by the state legislature as the University of Louisiana, Tulane University privatized in 1884. It is the only American university to be converted from a state public institution to a private one.

- With 4,400 employees, Tulane is the largest employer in New Orleans and an integral part of the community. Although most of the university was closed in September 2005 as a result of Hurricane Katrina's damaging effects, many students returned to help renew the city. In May 2006, former Presidents George H. W. Bush and Bill Clinton were the graduation speakers, commending the students for coming back to Tulane and serving the community.

- In 2006, Tulane created the Newcomb College Institute to support women's education at the university. The institute is a recognition of the H. Sophie Newcomb Memorial College, Tulane's women's coordinate college and the first of its kind in the United States. Its closing created a controversy that ultimately was resolved in the courts.

- For the 2010–2011 academic year, Tulane received more applications than any other public or private university in the United States. It is a member of the Association of American Universities (AAU), a select group of the 63 leading research universities in the United States and Canada.

Summary of Change

In 2005, for the first time since the Civil War, Tulane University was forced to close its doors. After Hurricane Katrina, classes were cancelled for the fall semester. Faculty and staff members operated from scattered locations throughout the nation, and students were displaced to other universities. Only four months later, the university welcomed back approximately 90 percent of enrolled undergraduate students to a renewed campus—a result that would not have been possible without appropriate leadership from the recently restructured board.

In the aftermath of the storm, the trustees did not have to be told what to do. Within the first 10 days, the board convened for a conference call even though half its members were affected personally by the disaster. Despite their "gut instinct to shovel," as one insider described it, board members knew their place within the university structure and functioned in a policy capacity. The board met three times to lay out a recovery plan for the university. Tough decisions were questioned, challenged, and built on facts before being put into action. Tulane was back on its feet ahead of schedule as the spring semester began in January 2006.

Just a few years earlier, such an efficient response from the board may not have been possible. When Scott S. Cowen was appointed president in 1998, he concluded that board structure and practice could be holding the university back. Having recently turned down a top job at another well-known private university where he observed low board performance, Cowen—a scholar of corporate governance—came to Tulane because he saw the beginnings of positive change, despite some troubling characteristics.

Two board members, John E. Koerner III and Martin D. Payson, had similar concerns about the direction of Tulane's board. Chair John Koerner, an alumnus and New Orleans native, noted the lack of resemblance between the board and student body. Less than a fifth of board members lived outside of the New Orleans area, and the university was expanding its enrollment strategy to include a more national effort. The board was largely populated by emeritus trustees. Levels of giving were moderate. John Koerner realized that Tulane "needed to cast a wider net" in terms of board members.

Around the same time, Martin Payson began to challenge how the board traditionally appointed new members. A geographical outsider from New York and one of the few non-alumni members, he came to the board from the university's parents' council. In addition, some board members raised questions about the scope of information that was shared with the board. During the presidential search, the board decided to bring in a consultant to reconsider board procedures, including the outgoing chair's role as leader of the nominating committee.

Following the consultant's review, the board began to carry out changes that improved its relationship to the university and, in turn, its overall performance. These changes included enlarging the board from 25 to 35 members, redesigning the nominating process, developing explicit criteria for board composition, instituting board-member orientation and education, and changing some fundamental board structures (including term limits, voting rights, and committees). Since then, Tulane has taken deliberate measures to sustain a high-performing board. By Scott Cowen's definition, such a board is "really engaged in the life of the institution and focused on ensuring that the institution has the strategy to achieve its mission and vision, but [it also has] the metrics to measure it on an ongoing basis." Based on the board's response to Hurricane Katrina, Tulane fits its president's description.

UNIVERSITY OF DUBUQUE

Featured in Chapter 8

2011 Profile

Location:	Dubuque, Iowa
Enrollment:	1,900
Classification:	Private, doctoral
Operating Budget:	$45 million
Endowment:	$71 million
Board Members:	36

Quick Facts

- The institution, a professional university with a liberal arts focus, comprises the undergraduate college, the graduate school, and the theological seminary.
- In 2004, a $32-million gift from the family of Lester G. and Michael Lester Wendt established the Wendt Character Initiative, which is designed to establish a "culture of character" throughout the university. This distinctive program—firmly rooted in Dubuque's mission, values, and Presbyterian identity—includes a scholars program, lecture series, campuswide workshops, a library collection, and integration of ethics into the curriculum.
- The university is firmly within the Presbyterian tradition inspired by Adrian Van Vliet. The UD Theological Seminary includes a special program for preparing Native-American pastoral leaders, as well as an emphasis on leadership for small congregations and a pioneering online Master of Divinity degree that combines online and residential components.

Summary of Change

Situated on high ground in a historic Mississippi River town, surrounded by an attractive middle-class neighborhood, the University of Dubuque campus has undergone a splendid makeover. Its 1,900 students attend classes in renovated or newly constructed facilities, work out in a state-of-the-art recreation and wellness center, and study in a handsomely rebuilt and expanded library and science center. Over the past decade, the institution has moved from near bankruptcy, an aging physical plant, and declining enrollment to a solid financial position. Enrollment has more than tripled, and endowment has quadrupled. Board members and others committed to Dubuque's mission contributed $128 million to the "forever better" capital campaign to renovate facilities and strengthen academic programs.

What explains the dramatic transformation of a struggling private college into this thriving center of learning? Certainly board decisions became transition points that reversed the trajectory from decline to growth in size and quality.

First, despite a tempting offer to partner with a for-profit entity, the board looked to its roots and chose to remain loyal to its historic mission of educating students and pursuing excellence in scholarship in keeping with the Presbyterian tradition. In the words of a former board chair, the university needed to reject choices that were based on survival at any cost and instead focus on "becoming what we were created to be."

Second, upon the departure of the president, the board selected its seminary dean and a former pastor, Jeffrey F. Bullock, to lead the university. A quietly charismatic communicator, Jeffrey Bullock acknowledges that a competitive spirit is strongly etched in his DNA. The board has energetically engaged with him in defining ambitious aspirations to become "the best small Christian university," in a league with Hope College in Michigan and Luther College in Iowa.

Third, the board did not shy away from contentious issues. It fully supported the president in reducing programs and faculty substantially during the early stages of Dubuque's turnaround. The board engaged in an acrimonious, but necessary, legal battle with the college faculty, which insisted that it held ultimately governing authority. The board prevailed over this unusual interpretation of shared governance. Without those tough choices, Dubuque could not have survived.

Finally, the board endorsed an enrollment-management strategy that capitalized on the tenor of the campus expressed in the Wendt Character Initiative, a unique program about "developing good character in community with others" that includes students, faculty members, and staff members. The enrollment strategy—led by an exceptionally talented management team—builds on Dubuque's blend of humanities and professional study. The university knows its audience and targets students who can profit from what Dubuque has to offer.

The University of Dubuque continues to grow in enrollment and to expand its programs. At this writing, the board is contemplating a $60-million building expansion, including a privately funded arts center and three new residence halls.

UNIVERSITY OF NORTH CAROLINA

Featured in Chapter 7

2011 Profile

Campuses:	16 universities and one residential high school
Enrollment:	222,000
Faculty and Staff:	44,000
Operating Budget:	$2 billion
State Funding:	$577 million
Board Members:	32

Quick Facts

- The University of North Carolina traces its beginnings to 1789, when the state's General Assembly chartered the University of North Carolina in Chapel Hill. "Carolina" is the first public university, and for 136 years it was UNC's only campus. By 1971, UNC had become a large, diverse, modern university system. It now accommodates all public baccalaureate and higher-level institutions in the state, including five historically black colleges and universities and one university chartered as a teacher's college for Lumbee Indians.

- The board of governors has 32 voting members elected by the General Assembly for four-year terms and one nonvoting student member. The board oversees the system as a whole, selects the system president, confirms the president's nomination of each campus chancellor, and approves the system budget. It delegates measured authority to campus boards of trustees.

- Owing in part to the political intricacy of its governance system and the diversity of regional, racial, and economic loyalties surrounding its universities, the board of governors has sought strong executives. William C. Friday (1956–1986) is credited with establishing a system known for competitive academics, strong central control balanced by respect for diverse campus missions and traditions, and rapport with the public.

Summary of Change

North Carolina's traditions of loyalty to an alma mater run deep. Chapel Hill occupies a special place in the hearts of its graduates, many of whom hold influential positions in business, government, and politics in the Tar Heel state. Alumni also hold strong allegiances to the state's other institutions. One challenge facing UNC system leaders has been aligning the competing loyalties and interests that surround its 16 universities with the statewide goal of strengthening economic opportunity. The University of North Carolina Tomorrow program attempts to forge this alliance.

When President Erskine Bowles stepped down in 2010, he left this change initiative as his signature accomplishment. His successor Thomas W. Ross, president of Davidson College and a former state superior court judge and foundation executive, will be responsible for moving UNC Tomorrow from blueprint to reality.

UNC Tomorrow, which began in 2007, is an ambitious plan to align university priorities with what residents view as their state's most pressing needs. While most systems seek public input on their way to developing strategic plans, UNC Tomorrow stands out for its participatory process. A 28-member commission of distinguished citizens, including 10 members of the board of governors, oversaw the effort. Chair Jim W. Phillips Jr. also chaired the commission, and Erskine Bowles participated in virtually every major meeting and community session. Faculty involvement came through a 14-member scholars council, and 1,000 members of the academic community contributed ideas in other ways. More than 10,000 people participated in the 11 Community Listening Forums, responded to surveys, or otherwise made their voices heard. This grassroots base is consistent with Erskine Bowles's view of the university as "a supply-driven organization that needs to turn itself into a demand-driven enterprise." The purpose of the statewide forums was to learn what citizens wanted their system to deliver, yet this massive display of local interest also reflects the historically close ties between North Carolinians and their university system.

UNC Tomorrow articulates what the universities can do to support the state's ability to compete in a global marketplace. About 33 percent of North Carolina's college-age students are enrolled in college—only 69 percent of the rate in South Korea. North Carolina also lags behind Greece, Finland, Belgium, Ireland, and Poland. The means to achieving the state's economic agenda is education: better access, improved teacher preparation, and more research with commercial potential. The recommendations clustered around seven priorities designed to direct future university strategies:

1. Improve the state's readiness to compete in global markets.
2. Increase access to higher education, especially for minority, immigrant, low-income, and other underrepresented groups.
3. Improve public education largely through better teacher preparation and in-service programs.
4. Contribute to economic development through applied research.
5. Strengthen the overall health of the state.
6. Improve environmental sustainability, especially in the university's energy usage.
7. Become more engaged with the economic, social, and cultural life of the state.

Early indicators suggest that this change agenda is starting to serve the UNC system well. In 2008–2009, North Carolina ranked first among 16 states in the Southern Regional Education Board in state appropriations per student and near the top in faculty salaries.

UNIVERSITY OF NORTH FLORIDA

Featured in Chapter 8

2011 Profile

Location:	Jacksonville, Fla.
Enrollment:	16,320
Classification:	Public, master's
Operating Budget:	$232 million
Endowment:	$70 million
Board Members:	13

Quick Facts

- UNF is one of 11 public institutions in the State University System of Florida, smaller than the research institutions—the University of Florida and Florida State University—but larger and more comprehensive than Florida Gulf Coast University and the University of West Florida.

- Located on a 1,300-acre campus halfway between downtown Jacksonville and the Atlantic beaches, UNF is graced by acres of nature preserve that incorporate small lakes and the indigenous flora and fauna of north Florida. The campus also has several new signature buildings.

- Three times over the past five years, the *Princeton Review* has ranked UNF as a Best Value College. It has also named UNF's Coggin College of Business as one of the 282 best business schools in the country.

- In 2010, UNF received the Community Engagement Classification from the Carnegie Foundation for the Advancement of Teaching. Based on U.S. State Department data, UNF students travel abroad for credit at twice the national average, giving them numerous opportunities to engage in what UNF terms "transformational learning."

- UNF athletic programs joined NCAA Division I in 2009.

Summary of Change

Chair R. Bruce Taylor and President John A. Delaney pursued a highly systematic approach to taking the institution to the next level. They began by spending considerable time in dialogue with the board and the campus community on what exactly that aspiration should be. They and other senior leaders visited potential peers, including Miami University in Ohio, the University of North Carolina at Wilmington, and The College of New Jersey. Based on this research, the board and president developed a complete set of measures to compare UNF's current and past performance and to evaluate its performance against its aspirational peers.

Even before the university began the exercise of targeting its destination, it had developed several signature programs. Transformational Learning Opportunities (TLOs) enable many students to engage in educational experiences that resemble those of a private liberal arts college, such as internships, international study, and service learning in the community. In keeping with its commitment to serving the region, UNF established flagship academic programs that deliver research and advance education in areas that are especially important to Jacksonville and northeast Florida: transportation and logistics, international business, community nursing, and coastal biology.

In a new mission, vision, and values statement, the board articulated the university's aspiration to offer regional service at a national level of quality. The board adjusted its own decision-making processes to enable board members to become more engaged with the university and more attentive to the strategies for reaching this goal. A revised approach to board meetings includes more interaction with faculty members and students, more opportunities to discuss future directions with the president, closer attention to UNF's well-developed set of metrics for assessing its progress, and more time on task.

UNIVERSITY SYSTEM OF MARYLAND

Featured in Chapter 7

2011 Profile		
	Campuses:	12 institutions and two regional higher education centers
	Enrollment:	152,497
	Faculty:	13,539
	Operating Budget:	$4.4 billion
	State Funding:	$1.1 billion
	Board Members:	17

Quick Facts

- The University System of Maryland (USM) is a large, complex organization with a diverse set of institutions: the flagship university at College Park; 10 other universities, including three minority-serving institutions and a "meta" university with elements of a liberal arts college and a research institution; and two regional learning centers that provide working Marylanders with access to USM resources.

- The system's board of regents has 17 members appointed by the governor and confirmed by the state senate (including the secretary of agriculture, who serves ex officio) and one student. The appointed regents serve five-year terms, and the student regent serves a one-year term, all with a limit of two consecutive terms. The board has responsibility for the overall management of the system, hiring the chancellor, and appointing presidents of the institutions (in consultation with the chancellor). The system board maintains a set of advisory councils (presidents, faculty members, staff members, and students) and committees.

- Since its founding in 1947 to serve students in the U.S. Military, University College (UMUC) has established itself as the largest university serving the military in the United States and at 23 centers around the globe.

Summary of Change

In 2003–2004, the regents initiated the comprehensive Effectiveness and Efficiency Initiative, intended to preserve and build institutional quality; accommodate more students; increase access for all, including historically underserved populations; curb tuition increases, and show the legislature and the public that the system merited their support. What is most remarkable about the regents' achievement is that the E&E Initiative has measurably reduced operating costs and held the line on tuition while educating more students for the state of Maryland. Bringing this kind of measurable change to a large system of over 150,000 students and 12 institutions is a major achievement, justly described in *Washington Monthly* as "A Mid-Atlantic Miracle."

The board chair and chancellor appointed a work group, designed as an ongoing entity "with the freedom and authority to review all aspects of the university system's operations." The E&E Initiative took on some of the most intractable features of the academy, including faculty workload, time to degree, and differentiated campus funding. For example, the initiative determined that faculty at the research universities should teach, on average, 5.5 course units, while their colleagues at the non-research "comprehensive" institutions should strive for a 7.5-unit course load. The faculty met or surpassed both goals.

To halt the phenomenon of "credit creep," in which degree requirements inch ever upward, forcing students to spend additional semesters on campus to complete their studies, the board mandated a strict 120-credit-hour limit (with a few exceptions when accreditation policies dictated otherwise). To respond to enrollment demand without a parallel increase in cost, undergraduate applicants were directed to lower-cost comprehensive universities over the more expensive research institutions. Three universities—Towson, Salisbury, and Bowie State—and University College, with its flexible, distance-education options, were designated as growth institutions and received special funding to accommodate additional students.

Had the regents merely laid out these goals as desirable aspirations, they would have found plenty of company in other public and private higher-education boardrooms. What sets the University System of Maryland apart is the follow-through that led to measurable and sometimes dramatic progress. By 2010, the Effectiveness and Efficiency Initiative had produced the following results:

- More than $200 million in cost savings have been achieved.
- The average graduation rate—now less than four and one-half years—exceeds those of most public systems by a substantial margin.
- In-state undergraduate tuition did not increase between the 2006 and 2009 academic years and increased by only 3 percent in 2010. Maryland's tuition, once the sixth highest of all public universities, is expected to rank 21st in 2011.
- Enrollment since the start of E&E has increased by 15,000 without supplemental state financial support.
- Several USM institutions are among the "top gainers" in minority graduation rates, and the African-American graduate rate at Towson University is nearly 70 percent—a few points above that of the whole university.

National rankings continue to list several USM institutions among the "best values" in higher education and as having many top-25 programs. One would be hard pressed to find another system or, for that matter, large institution that could match this list of important changes achieved in the relatively short span of six years.

UNIVERSITY OF WISCONSIN SYSTEM

Featured in Chapter 7

2011 Profile

Campuses:	13 four-year universities, 13 two-year colleges, and statewide UW-Extension
Enrollment:	182,090
Faculty and Staff:	33,486
Operating Budget:	$5.59 billion
State Funding:	$1.179 billion
Board Members:	18

Quick Facts

- The current University of Wisconsin System resulted from a merger in 1971 of the University of Wisconsin, which included the original land-grant university in Madison, and Wisconsin State Universities, which included the state teachers colleges.

- An 18-member board of regents oversees the system. The board includes 14 regents appointed by the governor for seven-year terms, two ex officio regents (the state superintendent of public instruction and the president or a designee of the Wisconsin Technical College System Board), and two student regents who serve two-year terms. The Wisconsin system is highly centralized. The regents appoint the system president and campus chancellors, as well as the deans of the two-year colleges.

- The flagship campus in Madison is widely regarded as a strong public research university. The regional campuses are viewed in the higher-education field as among the best of their kind for solid, traditional academic programs. The system also includes the state's extension service and Wisconsin Public Broadcasting.

Summary of Change

The challenge facing the University of Wisconsin System, and the state as a whole, is crystallized in an invidious comparison. In 2007, Minnesotans earned an average of $41,000, ranking 11th nationally in per capita income. Residents of Wisconsin—a state of similar size with the same mean temperatures and an equally extensive higher-education system—earned $36,000 on average and ranked 25th in per capita income. Minnesota surpasses Wisconsin in preparing its population for success in a knowledge economy and enjoys a substantially greater per-capita income. Wisconsin's economy historically rested on agriculture and heavy industry. Unlike Minnesota, it has come late to the work of aligning its higher-education system with preparing a workforce ready for a globally competitive economy.

Against this backdrop, Wisconsin's board of regents encouraged Kevin P. Reilly, the system's president, to take the system in a new direction and looked to him to articulate the vision. The question facing Reilly, the regents, and state leaders became, "How can Wisconsin at least match Minnesota in producing more graduates, building a stronger economy, and creating more and better-paying jobs?"

In response, Reilly rolled out the Growth Agenda for Wisconsin, a major reorientation of this large, stable system. The priorities are similar to those in other states seeking to spur economic development:

1. Better prepare students for the global economy and society.
2. Enroll and graduate more, and more-diverse, students in less time.
3. Apply university research to stimulate higher-wage jobs.
4. Use the universities as a nucleus to build stronger communities.
5. Grow net system resources.
6. Improve operational flexibility, efficiency, and effectiveness.
7. Increase partnership within the system and with external agencies.

Referring to the genesis of the Growth Agenda, Regent Mark Bradley observed: "Kevin conceived it [and] … the regents implemented it." In the face of some legislative cynicism, the regents and Reilly made the case for this change in direction from an institution-centric system to one focused on the needs of Wisconsin. They were persuasive. The university system received additional state funding for the Growth Agenda.

This strong academic culture was not naturally inclined toward putting its shoulder to the wheel of state economic development. But perhaps the most significant accomplishment of the regents' Growth Agenda for Wisconsin has been its focus on using university assets to shift Wisconsin's manufacturing and agriculturally based economy to one grounded more in high-growth, knowledge-based industries.

While this three-year-old initiative is too young to have done much to change the state's educational and economic profile, early returns are both sobering and promising. The system's candid Accountability Report 2009—2010 shows that the campuses fell short of their goals for retention and minority participation rates but met overall enrollment targets. In addition, the system has met or exceeded its goals in graduating more students overall and in increasing production in the science, technology, engineering, and math (STEM) fields.

WIDENER UNIVERSITY

Featured in Chapter 3

2011 Profile

Location:	Chester, Pa.
Enrollment:	3,275 undergraduate; 3,275 postgraduate
Classification:	Private, doctoral
Operating Budget:	$184.6 million
Endowment:	$70.4 million
Board Members:	25

Quick Facts

- Widener was founded in 1821 and has undergone several name changes. It was known as Pennsylvania Military College after 1892 and adopted the Widener name in 1972.

- An innovative, metropolitan university that combines academic quality with career preparation and a commitment to community service, Widener has its main campus 15 miles south of Philadelphia. It also maintains campuses in Exton and Harrisburg, Pa., and Wilmington, Del. The Harrisburg and Wilmington campuses offer law degrees.

- Widener has gained national recognition for its civic initiatives. It is one of only 22 colleges that are members of Project Pericles, an organization promoting social responsibility and addressing civic apathy among students. *Washington Monthly* ranked Widener among the top 100 national universities in its annual college rankings, which measure contribution to the public good.

- The university is home to flourishing Army ROTC and nursing programs. About 25 percent of students in the ROTC program are nursing majors. The university produced more Army nurses than any other institution in the 2006–2007 academic year.

Summary of Change

Chester, Pa., is a once-thriving town outside Philadelphia that is now seen as a poster child for urban decay, burdened by high crime rates and a school system that is reported to be the worst in the area. Widener University calls this struggling city home.

For much of its modern history, Widener walled itself off from its blighted surroundings. The city's reputation could be a detriment to enrollment and harm the institution's competition with other nearby institutions, including Swarthmore College, West Chester University, Villanova University, St. Joseph's University, Drexel University, Temple University, and University of Pennsylvania. Farsighted board members came to realize, however, that ignoring the neighborhood was a self-defeating strategy and unfair to the Chester community. The board decided to turn the location from a liability into an asset by nurturing a culture of civic engagement between campus and city. Rather than isolating itself from its troubled neighborhood, the institution would focus on becoming a catalyst for positive community change.

The board deliberately sought a new president who would forge bonds between the academy and the neighborhood. When current president James T. Harris joined Widener in 2002, he came ready to take action. In his previous position at Defiance College in Ohio, Jim Harris had a reputation for building bridges between the college and surrounding communities and made it clear to the board his intention to bring that same attitude to Widener. The board also began to change its structure to fit the university's new socially cognizant priorities. They created a civic-engagement committee, gave it substantive responsibilities for overseeing change, and named as its chair the director of the civic-engagement research center at neighboring University of Pennsylvania.

The board set a new tone for the university: civic engagement now lies at the core of its identity and academic programs. Even when faculty members pushed back with the concern that structural changes emphasized experiential learning over academics, the board stood by its principles and supported Jim Harris's actions. Since then, the board is doing the less dramatic but essential work of monitoring and evaluating performance.

Today, Widener is prospering. Enrollment is at nearly 7,000 students and among the highest in its history; the endowment of $58 million is recovering from the effects of the recession; and new retail development on university property near the main campus in Chester is generating net income and slowly improving neighborhood appearances. Rather than ignoring the problems of its hometown, Widener has found a way to become a positive part if its community and meet the needs of one of the most beleaguered cities in the country.

RESOURCES

AGB Statement on Board Responsibility for Institutional Governance. Washington, DC: Association of Governing Boards of Universities and Colleges, 2010.

Agnese, Louis J. "Repositioning for Success: Marketing, Enrollment Management and Innovative Financing Bring a College into the Future." Ed. Allen P. Splete, *Presidential Essays: Success Stories: Strategies that Make a Difference at Thirteen Independent Colleges and Universities.* New Agenda Series, Vol. 2, No. 2. Indianapolis, IN: USA Group, Inc., 2000.

Alinsky, Saul. *Rules for Radicals.* New York, NY: Random House, 1971.

Chabotar, Kent John. *Strategic Finance: Planning and Budgeting for Boards, Chief Executives, and Finance Officers.* Washington, DC: Association of Governing Boards of Universities and Colleges, 2006.

Chait, Richard; William P. Bryan; Barbara E. Taylor. *Governance as Leadership: Reframing the Work of Nonprofit Boards.* Hoboken, NJ: Wiley, 2004.

Clark, Timothy R. *Epic Change: How to Lead Change in the Global Age.* San Francisco, CA: Jossey-Bass, 2007.

Collins, Jim. *Good to Great: Why Some Companies Make the Leap ... and Others Don't.* New York, NY: HarperCollins Publishers Inc., 2001.

Collins, Jim. *Good to Great and the Social Sectors: A Monograph to Accompany Good to Great.* New York, NY: HarperCollins Publishers Inc., 2005.

Effective Governing Boards. Washington, DC: Association of Governing Boards of Universities and Colleges, 2009 and 2010.

Heifetz, Ronald. *Leadership Without Easy Answers.* Cambridge, MA: Harvard University Press, 1998.

Immerwahr, John and Jean Johnson. "Squeeze Play 2010: Continued Public Anxiety on Cost, Harsher Judgments on How Colleges are Run." San Jose, CA: The National Center for Public Policy and Higher Education, February 2010.

Kotter, John. *Leading Change.* Boston, MA: Harvard Business School Press, 1996.

MacTaggart, Terrence, ed. *Academic Turnarounds: Restoring Vitality to Challenged American Colleges and Universities.* Westport, CT: Praeger, 2007.

MacTaggart, Terrence. *Seeking Excellence through Independence: Liberating Colleges and Universities from Excessive Regulation.* San Francisco, CA: Jossey-Bass, 1998.

McGuinness, Aims. "A Model for Successful Restructuring." Ed. Terrence MacTaggart and Associates, *Restructuring Higher Education: What Works and What Doesn't in Reorganizing Governing Systems.* San Francisco, CA: Jossey-Bass, 1996.

Nadler, David. *Champions of Change: How CEOs and Their Companies are Mastering the Skills of Radical Change.* San Francisco, CA: Jossey-Bass, 1997.

Penson, Edward. *Board and President: Facilitating the Relationship.* Washington, DC: American Association of State Colleges and Universities, 1995.

Sonnenfeld, Jeffrey A. "What Makes Great Boards Great." *Harvard Business Review,* September 2002.

Strategic Imperatives: New Priorities for Higher Education. Washington, DC: Association of Governing Boards of Universities and Colleges, 2009.

"The Leadership Imperative: The Report of the AGB Task Force on the State of the Presidency in American Higher Education." Washington, DC: Association of Governing Boards of Universities and Colleges, 2006.

"Top Public Policy Issues for Higher Education in 2011 and 2012." Washington, DC: Association of Governing Boards of Universities and Colleges, 2011.

Additional resources are available at www.agb.org.

ABOUT THE AUTHOR

Terrence MacTaggart

Terry MacTaggart is an experienced leader and scholar in higher education. His consulting and research focuses on college and university leadership and policy, strategic planning, institutional advancement, board development, and leadership evaluation. He has served as a faculty member and administrator at several public and independent colleges and universities, where he has led or participated in substantial institutional transformations. He has held the chancellor's position at the Minnesota State University System and on two occasions at the University of Maine System. He has served as a consultant and facilitator for more than 200 colleges, universities, and systems.

His research and publications focus on governance, improving relations between institutions and the public, and restoring institutional vitality. His most recent book is *Academic Turnarounds: Restoring Growth and Vitality to Challenged American Colleges and Universities* (ACE/Praeger, 2007). With James Mingle, he authored *Pursuing the Public's Agenda: Trustees in Partnership with State Leaders* (AGB, 2002). He served as editor and lead author of *Restructuring Public Higher Education: What Works and What Doesn't in Reorganizing Public Systems* (Jossey-Bass, 1996). Two years later, he produced *Seeking Excellence Through Independence: Liberating Colleges and Universities from Excessive Regulation* (Jossey-Bass, 1998), which focuses on rebalancing campus autonomy and accountability in order to achieve better results. With Robert Berdahl, he wrote "Charter Colleges: Balancing Freedom and Accountability" (Pioneer Institute for Public Policy Research, 2000), a study of the partial privatization of public institutions.